CALVIN DANILO

Toronto On A Budget 2025

Exploring the Best of the City Without Breaking the Bank.

Copyright © 2024 by Calvin Danilo

All rights reserved. No part of this publication may be reproduced, stored or transmitted in any form or by any means, electronic, mechanical, photocopying, recording, scanning, or otherwise without written permission from the publisher. It is illegal to copy this book, post it to a website, or distribute it by any other means without permission.

Calvin Danilo asserts the moral right to be identified as the author of this work.

First edition

This book was professionally typeset on Reedsy.
Find out more at reedsy.com

Contents

Disclaimer	vii
Welcome to Toronto	viii
Why Visit Toronto on a Budget?	viii
Best Time to Visit: How to Save on Seasonal Travel	xi
Essential Packing Tips for Budget Travelers	xiii
Travel Smart: Safety and Budget Tips	xvi
Getting to Toronto	1
Budget-Friendly Flights and Arrival Options	1
Navigating Toronto Pearson International Airport	4
UP Express (Union Pearson Express)	7
TTC (Toronto Transit Commission) Bus and Subway	8
Airport Shuttle Services	8
Ride Shares (Uber, Lyft, etc.)	9
Taxis	10
Which Option is Best for You?	11
Getting Around Toronto	12
The Toronto Transit Commission (TTC): How to Use Public Transport on a Budget	12
Presto Card and Fare Passes: Maximize Savings on Transportation	14
Maximizing Savings with Fare Passes	16
TTC and Accessibility	17
Where the TTC Can Take You	17
Exploring Toronto by Foot: Walking-Friendly Routes	18
Budget Tips for Taxis, Rideshares, and Bike Rentals	21
Affordable Accommodations	24

Best Budget Hotels in Toronto	24
Hostels for Solo Travelers and Backpackers	26
Short-Term Rentals and Airbnb: How to Find Affordable Stays	29
University Dorms and Summer Housing Options	32
Tips for Booking University Dorms	34
Tips for Getting Last-Minute Accommodation Deals	35
Dining on a Budget	**41**
Cheap Eats in Toronto: Neighborhoods with Affordable Food	41
Best Street Food and Food Trucks: Quick and Budget-Friendly Meals	44
Top Budget Restaurants: Chinatown, Little Italy, and More	46
Markets for Cheap Eats: St. Lawrence Market and Kensington Market	49
Budget-Friendly Vegetarian and Vegan Options	51
Budget-Friendly Attractions	**56**
Free Attractions and Sights in Toronto	56
Museums and Galleries with Free or Discounted Entry	59
Exploring Toronto's Parks: High Park, Toronto Islands, and More	62
Free Walking Tours and Scenic Routes	67
Budget Tips for Iconic Landmarks	69
Shopping on a Budget	**76**
Budget Shopping Districts: Kensington Market, Queen Street West	76
Vintage Shops and Thrift Stores for Unique Bargains	78
Where to Find Local Art, Crafts, and Souvenirs on a Budget	81
Shopping Deals: Discount Outlets and Seasonal Markets	84
Nightlife and Entertainment	**87**
Affordable Bars and Lounges in Toronto	87

Free Outdoor Concerts and Festivals: Enjoy Toronto's Music Scene	90
Indie Theaters and Cinemas with Discount Tickets.	93
Budget-Friendly Nightclubs and Live Music Venues	96
Free and Low-Cost Evening Activities	99
Day Trips on a Budget	**105**
Day Trips from Toronto: Niagara Falls, Hamilton, and More	105
Affordable Transportation for Day Trips: GO Trains and Buses	109
Budget-Friendly Nature Escapes: Hiking Trails and Parks	111
Nearby Small Towns Worth Visiting on a Budget	115
Budget Itineraries	**118**
1-Day Budget Itinerary: Exploring Toronto on Foot	118
3-Day Budget Itinerary: Top Attractions and Free Activities	120
5-Day Itinerary: A Full Week of Budget-Friendly Adventures	124
Custom Itinerary Tips: Tailor Your Visit on a Budget	129
Entertainment and Fun	**132**
Free Festivals and Public Events: What to Look for in 2025	132
Budget-Friendly Cultural Experiences: Theater, Art, and Music	135
Sports on a Budget: Toronto Blue Jays and Raptors Game Day Tips	138
Cheap Movie Nights and Affordable Cinemas	141
General Tips for Budget Entertainment in Toronto	143
Outdoor Adventures: Kayaking, Biking, and More on a Budget	144
Tips for Saving on Outdoor Gear Rentals	149
Toronto for Families on a Budget	**151**
Family-Friendly Accommodations: Hotels and Rentals with Budget Options	151
Free and Cheap Activities for Kids	154

Top Parks and Playgrounds for Families	158
Budget Dining Options for Families	162
Tips for Traveling with Kids on a Budget	164
Toronto for Solo Travelers	**172**
Safe and Affordable Neighborhoods for Solo Travelers	172
Meeting Other Travelers: Budget-Friendly Social Experiences	175
Best Hostels for Solo Adventurers	179
Cheap Cafés and Bars for Solo Dining	182
Solo Travel Safety Tips for Toronto	185
Money-Saving Tips	**191**
Finding Discounts and Coupons for Attractions	191
How to Score Cheap Tickets to Major Events	194
Budget Tip Summary	198
Budget Travel Apps You Need in Toronto	198
Best Websites for Deals on Food, Entertainment, and Stays	202
Saving Money on Groceries and Essentials in Toronto	205
Essential Info	**213**
Emergency Contacts for Budget Travelers	213
Internet Access and Budget-Friendly SIM Cards	220
Conclusion	**226**

Disclaimer

This book is designed to be a trustworthy companion for your travels, providing in-depth insights and practical advice to make your journey smoother and more enjoyable. While every effort has been made to ensure the information is accurate at the time of writing, please note that local circumstances and travel details may evolve over time.

This guide is focused entirely on delivering useful, relevant content without images or maps. The aim is to offer comprehensive information to help you plan and experience a fulfilling trip.

Use this guide as your foundation, and let your adventures shape the rest of your story.

Welcome to Toronto

Why Visit Toronto on a Budget?

Toronto is known for being one of Canada's major cities, but that doesn't mean it has to be expensive. There are many things to do for free or at low cost, especially if you know where to look. From parks to museums to markets, you can enjoy Toronto without breaking the bank.

Free and Affordable Attractions

High Park (1873 Bloor St W, Toronto, ON M6R 2Z3)

- This is the city's largest public park, offering free activities like hiking, picnicking, and even a small zoo that's open all year round. The park is especially nice in the spring when cherry blossoms bloom. Take a walk around the gardens, and don't forget to check out the Grenadier Pond.
- Cost: Free
- How to get there: Take the TTC subway to High Park Station.

Toronto Islands (9 Queens Quay W, Toronto, ON M5J 2H3)

- A quick and cheap ferry ride from downtown will take you to the Toronto Islands, where you can enjoy beaches, bike rides, and walks with great views of the city skyline. It's a great spot for budget travelers who want to escape the city's hustle for a few hours.

- Ferry Cost: $8.70 CAD round trip for adults.
- How to get there: Ferries leave from the Jack Layton Ferry Terminal.

Art Gallery of Ontario (AGO) (317 Dundas St W, Toronto, ON M5T 1G4)

- This museum is free on Wednesdays from 6 p.m. to 9 p.m., making it a great budget-friendly option. You can see thousands of artworks from across the world, including Canadian artists.
- Cost: Free on Wednesdays, otherwise $25 CAD for general admission.
- How to get there: Take the subway to St. Patrick Station.

St. Lawrence Market (93 Front St E, Toronto, ON M5E 1C3)

- This is one of Toronto's most famous markets. Even if you're not buying anything, it's a great place to walk around and soak up the local culture. You can also pick up cheap eats from vendors, with options like peameal bacon sandwiches that are famous in the city.
- Cost: Free to visit, food prices vary.
- How to get there: Take the subway to King Station, then a short walk east.

Kensington Market

- Kensington Market is one of the most diverse neighborhoods in Toronto. It's filled with vintage shops, street art, and inexpensive places to eat. You can wander around the streets for free, enjoying the colorful vibe and maybe pick up a cheap snack from one of the local vendors.
- Cost: Free to explore, food prices vary.
- How to get there: Take the TTC to Spadina Station and walk south.

Distillery District (55 Mill St, Toronto, ON M5A 3C4)

- This historic area is perfect for a budget traveler who enjoys walking through quaint streets. The Distillery District is full of art galleries, cafes, and boutiques. It's free to explore, and there are often art installations or free events happening, especially around the holidays.
- Cost: Free to enter, prices for shops and cafes vary.
- How to get there: Take the 504 King Streetcar.

Nathan Phillips Square (100 Queen St W, Toronto, ON M5H 2N2)

- A must-see spot for budget travelers. In the winter, the square features free outdoor skating. During the summer, there are free concerts and events. Plus, the Toronto sign is an iconic photo spot.
- Cost: Free to explore; skate rental costs around $10 CAD.
- How to get there: Subway to Queen Station.

Affordable Food and Cheap Eats

Toronto has a huge range of budget-friendly food options, thanks to its diverse culture. You can enjoy different cuisines without spending a lot.

Banh Mi Boys (392 Queen St W, Toronto, ON M5V 2A9)

- Known for their Vietnamese banh mi sandwiches, this place offers tasty food at very reasonable prices. You can grab a sandwich for about $7 CAD.
- How to get there: Take the 501 Queen streetcar to Queen St West.

Seven Lives Tacos y Mariscos (69 Kensington Ave, Toronto, ON M5T 2K2)

- Located in Kensington Market, this taco spot is popular with locals. For about $6 CAD per taco, you get a generous portion, making it a great budget meal.
- How to get there: Take the TTC to Spadina Station and walk south.

Mother's Dumplings (421 Spadina Ave, Toronto, ON M5T 2G6)

- If you're craving Chinese food, this place serves large portions of dumplings at affordable prices. You can get a plate of handmade dumplings for around $10 CAD.
- How to get there: Take the TTC to Spadina Station.

Taverne Tamblyn (423 Danforth Ave, Toronto, ON M4K 1P1)

- A great spot for cheap drinks and snacks on the Danforth. You can get pints of local beer for about $5 CAD and enjoy their happy hour deals.
- How to get there: Take the subway to Pape Station.

Best Time to Visit: How to Save on Seasonal Travel

Spring (April to June)

Spring is a good time to visit because the weather is mild, and it's not too crowded. You can also find cheaper flights and hotel deals compared to the peak summer season. In spring, many of Toronto's outdoor activities, like parks and gardens, are open, making it easy to enjoy the city for free.

- **Events:** The **Cherry Blossom Festival** in High Park is a great free event in late April or early May. You can take in the beautiful trees in full bloom.

- **Costs:** Hotel prices in spring can be lower, especially in April and early May, starting around $100 CAD per night for budget hotels.
- **How to Save:** Many restaurants and attractions may offer spring deals before the busy summer season kicks in.

Summer (July to August)

Summer is the busiest time in Toronto, with lots of events and festivals. While it's a popular time to visit, it can be more expensive due to the influx of tourists. However, if you book in advance, you can still find deals, especially if you're looking to stay in hostels or short-term rentals.

- **Events: Canada Day** celebrations on July 1st offer free events and concerts across the city. **Harbourfront Centre** hosts many free outdoor performances in the summer.
- **Costs:** Expect higher prices for accommodation, starting around $150 CAD for budget hotels. However, public transport and free events can help keep your budget in check.
- **How to Save:** Take advantage of free festivals and events during the summer to enjoy music, food, and culture without spending extra.

Fall (September to November)

Fall is another great time to visit Toronto. The weather is cooler, but there are fewer tourists, which means you can often find cheaper flights and accommodation. The autumn foliage makes parks and outdoor areas especially nice to explore.

- **Events:** The **Toronto International Film Festival (TIFF)** takes place in September. While tickets can be expensive, you can often catch free screenings or outdoor events during the festival.
- **Costs:** Hotel prices drop again, especially after September, with budget options starting around $90 CAD per night.

- **How to Save:** Visit the city's parks and nature spots to enjoy the fall colors for free. Many attractions may also offer off-season discounts.

Winter (December to March)

Winter is the coldest time in Toronto, but it's also when you can find the best deals. If you're prepared to brave the cold, you can enjoy the city's winter festivals, ice skating, and Christmas markets.

- **Events:** The **Toronto Christmas Market** in the Distillery District is free to visit during the week. Skating at **Nathan Phillips Square** is another budget-friendly winter activity.
- **Costs:** Winter is the cheapest time for flights and hotels, with rooms as low as $70 CAD per night in January and February.
- **How to Save:** Bundle up and enjoy free or low-cost winter activities, like ice skating and holiday markets.

Essential Packing Tips for Budget Travelers

1. Clothing and Weather Gear

Toronto has four distinct seasons, and each requires different gear. Depending on when you visit, make sure to pack clothes that will keep you comfortable without having to spend on new ones once you arrive.

- **Winter (December to February):** If you're visiting during winter, it's cold, with temperatures often dropping below freezing. Pack a warm coat (preferably waterproof or at least resistant), thermal layers, gloves, a scarf, and a hat. You should also bring waterproof boots, as snow can make sidewalks slushy. Buying a coat or boots in Toronto can be expensive, so bring these items with you. You can expect to pay **$100+ CAD** for a decent winter coat in stores like **Winners** or **The Bay**.

- **Spring (March to May):** Toronto's spring is mild, but it can be rainy. Pack a light jacket or windbreaker, and don't forget a travel umbrella or a lightweight rain poncho. A poncho is more budget-friendly than buying an umbrella in Toronto (which can cost around **$10-15 CAD** at convenience stores).
- **Summer (June to August):** Summers are warm, but sometimes humid. Light, breathable clothing is ideal. Bring a reusable water bottle to stay hydrated. Most parks and public areas in Toronto have water fountains, so you can refill your bottle for free. This will save you from buying bottled water, which costs about **$2-3 CAD** at corner stores.
- **Fall (September to November):** Fall can be unpredictable, with both warm and chilly days. Layers are key. Pack a sweater or hoodie for cooler evenings and a jacket in case temperatures drop unexpectedly.

2. **Footwear**

Bring comfortable walking shoes, regardless of the season. Toronto is a very walkable city, and budget travelers will appreciate avoiding extra transit costs by exploring on foot. For those planning on hiking, such as a visit to the **Toronto Islands** or **High Park**, sturdy sneakers or hiking shoes are ideal. You don't want to waste money on emergency shoe purchases, which can be costly. Expect to pay **$50-150 CAD** for decent sneakers in stores like **Sport Chek** or **Foot Locker**.

3. **Reusable Items**

One of the best ways to save money while traveling is by avoiding single-use items. Not only does it save you money, but it's also environmentally friendly.

- **Reusable Water Bottle:** As mentioned earlier, Toronto has many places to refill a water bottle for free. Bringing your own can save you several dollars a day, which adds up over a trip.
- **Reusable Shopping Bag:** Toronto has a plastic bag fee, typically around

$0.05 CAD per bag at most grocery and convenience stores. A reusable bag is lightweight, easy to pack, and can save you from these small but annoying fees.

4. Travel-Sized Toiletries

Avoid buying full-sized toiletries at your destination, as these can cost more in tourist-heavy areas. Bring travel-sized shampoo, conditioner, body wash, and toothpaste from home. If you're staying in hostels or budget hotels that may not provide complimentary toiletries, packing your own essentials is crucial. Stores like **Shoppers Drug Mart** sell travel-sized toiletries, but they're pricier than in many other countries—expect to pay **$3-5 CAD** per item.

5. Portable Charger and Power Adapter

Toronto uses the standard North American electrical outlet (120V), so if you're coming from Europe, Asia, or other regions, bring a power adapter. A portable charger is essential because you'll likely rely on your phone for maps, transport apps, and staying connected with friends or family. Buying these items in Toronto can set you back **$20-50 CAD**, so it's best to pack them ahead of time.

6. Public Transport Essentials

Toronto's public transit system (TTC) is one of the most efficient ways to get around the city, especially for budget travelers. Pack a **Presto card** if you have one from a previous trip. If not, you can buy one when you arrive. A **Presto card** costs **$6 CAD** and can be loaded with funds for bus, streetcar, and subway rides, which are **$3.35 CAD** per trip. Consider purchasing a **day pass ($13.50 CAD)** or a **weekly pass ($43.75 CAD)** if you plan on using public transit often.

Travel Smart: Safety and Budget Tips

Toronto is generally a safe city, but as with any major destination, it's important to stay aware and follow some basic safety tips. Additionally, there are many ways to save money while keeping safe.

1. **Avoiding Tourist Traps**

   Certain areas of Toronto are more tourist-centric and can be overpriced. **Dundas Square** and **Harbourfront** are examples of places where food, drinks, and souvenirs can be more expensive due to their popularity. Instead, head a few blocks away from these areas to find cheaper local spots. For instance, while **Dundas Square** restaurants might charge **$15-20 CAD** for a meal, you can find budget-friendly options in **Kensington Market** or **Chinatown** for as little as **$7-10 CAD**.

2. **Use Public Transit Over Taxis**

   While Toronto taxis and rideshare services like **Uber** are available, they can be expensive, especially during peak hours. A taxi from the airport to downtown can cost you around **$60 CAD**. Instead, take the **UP Express** train, which costs **$12.35 CAD** and takes you directly from the airport to Union Station downtown in just 25 minutes. Another alternative is the **TTC airport bus**, which costs **$3.35 CAD** and connects you to the subway system.

3. **Explore Free Attractions**

   Toronto is home to many free attractions that can help you stretch your budget further. For instance, entry to **High Park**, Toronto's largest public park, is free. Here you can enjoy hiking trails, gardens, and even a free zoo. The **Toronto Islands** are another must-see and offer a great view of the city skyline. A round-trip ferry ticket to the islands costs **$8.70 CAD** (free for kids under 14), and once there, you can enjoy the beaches and picnic areas for free.

Other free spots include:

- **The Distillery District**, a historic area with beautiful cobblestone streets, art galleries, and cafes.
- **St. Lawrence Market**—it's free to enter, and you can browse the stalls even if you don't buy anything.
- **Nathan Phillips Square**, where you can snap a photo with the iconic Toronto sign.

4. Stay in Safe Areas

While Toronto is largely safe, some areas are better avoided late at night. Stick to well-lit, busy areas, particularly when walking alone. Neighborhoods like **Yorkville**, **The Annex**, and **Kensington Market** are known for being both budget-friendly and safe for travelers. Avoid isolated parks or areas that aren't well-trafficked after dark. If you feel unsure, use public transport or rideshare services to get back to your accommodation.

5. Budget Accommodations in Safe Neighborhoods

Staying in a good neighborhood doesn't have to break the bank. Consider budget-friendly areas like **The Annex, Cabbagetown,** or **Leslieville**. Hostels such as **Planet Traveler Hostel** or budget hotels like **The Rex Hotel** are great choices for saving money while being centrally located in safe areas. A night in a shared dorm at **Planet Traveler Hostel** costs around **$40-50 CAD**, while private rooms in budget hotels can range from **$80-120 CAD** per night.

6. Emergency Numbers and Travel Insurance

Always have emergency numbers saved in your phone, such as **911** for emergencies, and the number for your country's embassy. Also, consider getting travel insurance that covers health, accidents, and trip cancellations. Canada's healthcare system is excellent, but visitors will need to pay for medical services unless covered by insurance. A basic doctor's visit can cost

$100+ CAD, so it's worth investing in travel insurance before you arrive.

Getting to Toronto

Budget-Friendly Flights and Arrival Options

Finding affordable flights to Toronto can be easy if you plan ahead and know where to look. Toronto has two main airports: **Toronto Pearson International Airport (YYZ)** and the smaller **Billy Bishop Toronto City Airport (YTZ)**. Most international and larger flights come into Pearson, while Billy Bishop caters to regional flights and a few smaller international routes.

1. **Use Budget Airlines**

Toronto is served by several budget airlines that can help you save money, especially if you book early. Some of the most popular low-cost carriers flying into Toronto include:

- **WestJet**: A Canadian budget airline that offers domestic and international flights at lower prices compared to other full-service airlines. They frequently run sales and offer discounted fares, especially if you book several months in advance.
- **Flair Airlines**: Another Canadian low-cost carrier that offers super-cheap flights to Toronto from various cities in Canada and the United States. Their flights often have fewer frills, so you may need to pay extra for things like seat selection and checked baggage, but their base prices are often unbeatable.

- **Air Transat**: Known for cheap international flights, especially between Europe and Canada. If you're coming from Europe, Air Transat frequently offers sales and can be a great budget option for travelers headed to Toronto.
- **Swoop**: Owned by WestJet, Swoop offers ultra-low-cost flights within Canada and to select U.S. destinations. Keep an eye out for their flash sales, which sometimes offer flights as low as **$50 CAD**.

2. Best Times to Book

Timing is everything when booking a budget flight to Toronto. Prices fluctuate depending on the season and how far in advance you book.

- **Off-Peak Travel**: Flights are typically cheaper in the off-peak travel months of **January, February, and November**. These are colder months in Toronto, but if you're prepared for winter, you can save a significant amount on airfare.
- **Peak Travel**: The most expensive times to fly to Toronto are in the summer (**June to August**) and during the holiday season (**December**). If you must travel during these times, book your flights at least three to six months in advance to secure the best deals.
- **Midweek Flights**: Flights to Toronto are often cheaper if you fly midweek, especially on **Tuesdays and Wednesdays**. Weekend flights tend to be more expensive, especially on Fridays and Sundays when demand is higher.

3. Use Price Comparison Websites and Apps

Several websites and apps can help you find the cheapest flights to Toronto. Always compare prices across different platforms before booking to ensure you're getting the best deal.

- **Google Flights**: A very user-friendly platform that lets you compare

prices across airlines and filter flights by date, duration, and airline. You can also set up price alerts, so you'll get a notification when prices drop for flights to Toronto.
- **Skyscanner**: This platform is great for comparing flights from multiple budget airlines, including smaller carriers that may not show up on all search engines. Skyscanner also allows you to search for flights across a whole month to see which days are cheapest to fly.
- **Hopper**: An app that uses historical data to predict the best time to book your flight. Hopper will tell you whether to book now or wait for a better deal, making it useful for budget-conscious travelers.
- **Momondo**: This site is especially helpful for international travelers. It searches a wide range of airlines, including budget carriers, and often finds lower prices than larger sites like Expedia or Kayak.

4. Look for Flight Sales

Airlines often run flash sales where you can find amazing deals on flights to Toronto. These sales typically happen during off-peak seasons, but you can catch them year-round if you're lucky.

- **WestJet and Air Canada** frequently run sales during **Boxing Day (December 26th)**, **Black Friday**, and **Cyber Monday**.
- **Flair Airlines** and **Swoop** also offer seasonal promotions, where you can grab flights for as little as **$49 CAD** on select routes.

Sign up for airline newsletters or follow them on social media to stay in the loop on upcoming sales.

5. Baggage Fees and Extras

Many budget airlines charge extra for things like checked baggage, seat selection, and onboard meals. Be sure to factor these additional costs into your budget when comparing flights. For example:

- **Flair Airlines** charges around **$35-50 CAD** for a checked bag and **$10-15 CAD** for seat selection.
- **WestJet** and **Air Transat** have similar fees, so it's worth traveling light and only bringing a carry-on if possible. Most budget airlines allow one free carry-on, but be sure to check the size and weight restrictions beforehand to avoid surprise fees at the airport.

Navigating Toronto Pearson International Airport

Toronto Pearson International Airport (YYZ) is the main airport for most international and domestic flights. It's about **22.5 kilometers (14 miles)** from downtown Toronto, and there are several budget-friendly ways to get from the airport to your accommodation without overspending.

1. **UP Express Train**

One of the fastest and most affordable ways to get from Pearson Airport to downtown Toronto is by taking the **UP Express** (Union Pearson Express) train. The train departs from **Terminal 1** and goes directly to **Union Station** in downtown Toronto.

- **Cost**: A one-way ticket costs **$12.35 CAD** for adults and **$6.20 CAD** for seniors or students. Kids under 12 ride for free.
- **Travel Time**: The journey takes just **25 minutes**, making it one of the fastest options.
- **How to Get There**: The UP Express departs from **Terminal 1**, and there are clear signs directing you to the platform.
- **Ticket Purchase**: You can buy tickets at the station or online through the **UP Express website** or app.

For budget travelers staying in the downtown core, the UP Express is a great choice. It's fast, affordable, and reliable.

2. TTC Public Transit

Another budget option is to take the **TTC** (Toronto Transit Commission) bus and subway system. This is the cheapest way to get from Pearson Airport to downtown Toronto, though it does take a bit longer.

- **Route**: You can take the **192 Airport Rocket** bus from **Terminal 1** or **Terminal 3** to **Kipling Station** on the **Bloor-Danforth Subway Line**. From there, transfer to the subway heading east toward downtown Toronto.
- **Cost**: A single TTC fare is **$3.35 CAD**, and it includes transfers between buses and the subway.
- **Travel Time**: The trip to downtown Toronto takes about **60-90 minutes**, depending on your final destination.
- **How to Get There**: Look for TTC signs in the arrivals area. The 192 Airport Rocket bus picks up passengers outside both terminals.

The TTC is ideal for budget travelers who don't mind a longer journey and want to save a bit of money. Plus, you'll get a sense of the city's public transport system right away.

3. Ride-Share Services

If you're traveling with a group or have a lot of luggage, ride-share services like **Uber** and **Lyft** are available at Pearson Airport. While these are more expensive than public transit, they can still be a budget-friendly option if you split the cost with others.

- **Cost**: An Uber from Pearson to downtown Toronto will cost anywhere from **$40-60 CAD**, depending on the time of day and traffic.
- **How to Get There**: Follow the signs to the **Uber/Lyft pick-up area** located on the **Ground Level** of both terminals.

Ride-shares are a good middle ground for travelers who want convenience but don't want to pay for a taxi. Prices can fluctuate, so check the app before deciding.

4. **Airport Shuttle Services**

Many budget hotels and hostels offer free or low-cost shuttle services to and from Pearson Airport. Check with your accommodation ahead of time to see if this is an option.

- **Cost**: Some shuttles are free, while others may charge a small fee, usually between **$10-20 CAD**.
- **How to Get There**: Shuttles typically pick up passengers outside **Terminal 1** or **Terminal 3**. Look for the hotel shuttle pick-up zone.

This is a convenient option if you're staying at a hotel or hostel that offers it. Make sure to check with your hotel beforehand to confirm the shuttle schedule and pick-up location.

5. **Taxis**

Taxis are readily available at Pearson Airport, but they're one of the more expensive ways to get to downtown Toronto.

- **Cost**: A taxi to downtown Toronto will cost about **$60-75 CAD** depending on traffic.
- **How to Get There**: Taxi stands are located just outside the arrivals area at both **Terminal 1** and **Terminal 3**.

While taxis are the most expensive option, they're convenient if you're in a hurry or arriving late at night when public transit options may be limited.

UP Express (Union Pearson Express)

The **UP Express** is by far one of the quickest and most convenient options for budget travelers. It connects **Toronto Pearson International Airport** to **Union Station** in downtown Toronto. The train departs every 15 minutes from **Terminal 1**, and the ride takes just **25 minutes** to reach Union Station. This makes it one of the best choices if you're staying downtown or need to connect to other transportation from Union Station.

- **Cost:** One-way fare is **$12.35 CAD** for adults. Children under 12 ride for free.
- **Schedule:** Runs every 15 minutes from **5:30 AM** to **1:00 AM**, seven days a week.
- **Where to find it:** If you're landing at **Terminal 1**, follow the signs to the UP Express station. If you land at **Terminal 3**, you can take the free **Terminal Link Train** to get to Terminal 1.
- **Why choose this:** The UP Express is ideal if you're in a rush to get downtown. It's also the easiest if you're traveling with kids, as children under 12 ride free. However, it's not the cheapest option, especially if you're traveling with a large group of adults.

Address:
Toronto Pearson International Airport
6301 Silver Dart Dr, Mississauga, ON L5P 1B2
Contact: +1 416-776-3055 (Pearson Airport)
Union Station Contact: +1 888-438-6646 (UP Express)
Website: UP Express

TTC (Toronto Transit Commission) Bus and Subway

If you're looking for the cheapest way to get into the city, the **TTC** bus and subway system is your best bet. The **TTC airport bus** (Route 900) operates from **Pearson Airport's Terminal 1** to **Kipling Station**, which is on the **Line 2 Bloor-Danforth Subway**. From Kipling, you can connect to the subway system and travel across the city. Although it takes longer than the UP Express, it's much cheaper.

- **Cost:** One-way fare is **$3.35 CAD** if you use a **Presto card**, or **$3.25 CAD** if you pay cash. You can purchase a Presto card at the airport or use cash at the machine. Transfers between buses and subway lines are free as long as you complete your trip within a 2-hour window.
- **Schedule:** The TTC runs 24 hours a day, but service frequency varies. The **900 Airport Express** bus runs approximately every **10-15 minutes**.
- **Where to find it:** The TTC bus departs from **Terminal 1, Ground Level**, Column R4.
- **Why choose this:** This is the best option for budget-conscious travelers who don't mind spending a little more time on transit. It's also great if you're staying somewhere along the subway lines and don't need to go all the way to downtown. However, it's not the best if you have a lot of luggage or if you're traveling during rush hour, as it can get crowded.

TTC Contact: +1 416-393-4636
Website: TTC.ca

Airport Shuttle Services

Shuttle services are another good option for budget travelers, especially if you're not staying in the downtown core and need to get to one of the city's suburbs or other neighborhoods. Several private companies operate shuttle services, and some hotels also offer shuttles to and from the airport.

- **Cost:** Shuttle prices vary depending on the service provider and destination. Expect to pay around **$20-30 CAD** for a one-way trip.
- **Schedule:** Shuttle schedules depend on the company, but most services run every **30-60 minutes**. You may need to pre-book, so it's a good idea to arrange your shuttle ahead of time.
- **Where to find it:** You'll find shuttles at the **Ground Transportation area** at **Terminal 1** or **Terminal 3**. Follow the airport signs for "Ground Transportation."
- **Why choose this:** Shuttles are great if you're traveling with a group or need to get to a destination that isn't downtown. It's also a good option if you're staying in a hotel that offers a complimentary shuttle. However, shuttles can be slower than other forms of transport, especially if you have to wait for other passengers.

Popular Shuttle Providers:

- **Pearson Airport Limousine**: +1 416-776-3055
- **Toronto Airport Shuttle**: +1 416-777-2255
- **GO Airport Shuttle**: +1 905-670-7777

Ride Shares (Uber, Lyft, etc.)

If you prefer a more direct form of transportation, ride-share services like **Uber** and **Lyft** are available at Toronto Pearson. These services can be more affordable than taxis, but the price can vary depending on demand (such as during rush hour or bad weather). It's convenient, though, and you can easily arrange your ride through an app without needing to worry about cash.

- **Cost:** A ride from Pearson Airport to downtown Toronto typically costs

$35-45 CAD for a standard vehicle, though prices can surge during peak times.
- **Schedule:** Available 24/7, but surge pricing applies during high-demand periods.
- **Where to find it:** Ride-share pick-up zones are at **Terminal 1 (Ground Level, Door Q)** and **Terminal 3 (Arrivals Level, Door D).**
- **Why choose this:** Ride shares are ideal if you're traveling in a group and can split the cost or if you're heading somewhere that isn't well-connected by public transit. However, if you're a solo traveler on a tight budget, this may not be the best choice as costs can add up quickly.

Contact:
Uber Canada: Uber App
Lyft Canada: Lyft App

Taxis

While not the cheapest option, taxis are convenient and offer direct transportation from the airport to your accommodation. This is a good option if you have a lot of luggage, if you're arriving late at night, or if you just prefer not to deal with public transit. All taxis at the airport are licensed, and the fares are regulated by the airport authority, so you don't have to worry about overcharging.

- **Cost:** A taxi from Pearson Airport to downtown Toronto will cost you around **$60 CAD**. If you're traveling to a suburb or further area, expect to pay more.
- **Schedule:** Taxis are available 24/7.
- **Where to find it:** Taxis are available outside **Terminal 1** and **Terminal 3** in the **Ground Transportation area**.
- **Why choose this:** Taxis are the best option if you have a lot of luggage or if you're traveling with kids and need a bit more space. They're also

more convenient if you're arriving late or early when public transport is less frequent. But if you're on a tight budget, taxis may not be the best choice given the high cost.

Taxi Contacts:
Toronto Pearson Taxi Service: +1 416-776-3055
Beck Taxi: +1 416-751-5555
Diamond Taxi: +1 416-366-6868

Which Option is Best for You?

It all depends on what your priorities are. If you're on a tight budget and don't mind a longer travel time, the **TTC bus and subway** is your best bet at **$3.35 CAD** per trip. It's ideal if you're staying somewhere along the subway lines or don't have a lot of luggage. For those looking to get downtown quickly, the **UP Express** at **$12.35 CAD** is fast and convenient, but it's pricier.

If you're traveling in a group or need more comfort, **ride-shares** or **shuttles** may be more economical when you split the cost. And if convenience is your top priority, especially if you're traveling with children or a lot of luggage, **taxis** are a solid choice despite the higher cost.

Getting Around Toronto

The **Toronto Transit Commission (TTC)** is the city's main public transportation system, and for budget travelers, it's one of the best ways to get around Toronto. It covers the entire city through a network of buses, streetcars, and subway lines, making it easy and affordable to explore both downtown and the surrounding neighborhoods.

The Toronto Transit Commission (TTC): How to Use Public Transport on a Budget

The TTC operates with three main forms of transportation: buses, streetcars, and subways. Each option is well-connected, meaning you can easily transfer between them with just one fare, as long as you complete your journey within two hours. Here's a breakdown of how you can use the TTC on a budget:

1. **Buses**

The bus system covers areas that the subway doesn't reach. If you're staying outside of the downtown core, you'll likely find buses more convenient. They run frequently and connect with subway stations and streetcar routes. Each bus stop has a route number and direction clearly marked.

- **Cost:** One ride costs **$3.35 CAD** if you use a Presto card (more on that below), or **$3.25 CAD** if you pay in cash. Children under 12 ride for

free.
- **How to use:** When boarding, tap your Presto card on the green reader by the driver or drop exact change into the fare box. Bus drivers do not give change, so be sure to have the exact fare if you're paying cash.

Pro Tip: Some bus routes run 24 hours a day (like the **Blue Night Network**), which is helpful if you're out late and want to save on taxi or rideshare costs.

2. **Streetcars**

Toronto is famous for its streetcars, which are a convenient way to travel within the city, especially in areas like **King Street** and **Queen Street West**. Streetcars generally run on main roads and are easy to spot. Just wait at one of the streetcar stops, which are marked by TTC signs, and board through the front or middle doors.

- **Cost:** Same as the bus—**$3.35 CAD** with a Presto card or **$3.25 CAD** with cash.
- **How to use:** If you're using a Presto card, tap the green reader when you board. If you're paying cash, use the fare machine near the front door to pay and get a paper transfer if you need one.

Pro Tip: Streetcars can be slower during rush hour because they share the road with other vehicles. To avoid long waits, plan to use them during off-peak hours or stick to subways when you're in a rush.

3. **Subways**

The TTC subway system has four lines:

- **Line 1 (Yonge-University):** Runs north-south through downtown Toronto.
- **Line 2 (Bloor-Danforth):** Runs east-west.

- **Line 3 (Scarborough):** Covers the eastern parts of the city.
- **Line 4 (Sheppard):** Serves the northern areas.

Most budget travelers will use Lines 1 and 2, as these take you to popular destinations like **Union Station**, **Yonge-Dundas Square**, **Kensington Market**, and more.

- **Cost:** Same as buses and streetcars—**$3.35 CAD** with a Presto card or **$3.25 CAD** with cash.
- **How to use:** Tap your Presto card at the station gates or use a token if you prefer. Tokens can be purchased from vending machines in stations, but using a Presto card is easier for daily use.

Pro Tip: The subway system is the quickest way to get around, especially if you're traveling between major downtown areas. It's also great if you want to save money by staying in a budget hotel outside of the downtown core—just take the subway into the city center.

Presto Card and Fare Passes: Maximize Savings on Transportation

The **Presto card** is a contactless smart card that you can load with funds to pay for TTC fares. It's by far the most convenient and cost-effective way to travel around Toronto if you're using public transit frequently. Here's how it works and how it can save you money:

1. **Getting a Presto Card**
You can buy a Presto card at the following places:

- **TTC subway stations**: Presto vending machines are available at all subway stations.
- **Shoppers Drug Mart**: This popular Canadian pharmacy chain also

sells Presto cards. You'll find one in almost every neighborhood, making it easy to get a card soon after you arrive.
- **Online**: If you prefer, you can order a Presto card from their official website before your trip and have it delivered to your home. The card costs **$6 CAD**, plus any funds you want to load onto it.

Once you have your card, you can load it with funds either online, at a TTC station, or at participating retailers like **Shoppers Drug Mart**. You can add as little as **$10 CAD** to start.

Presto Card Cost:

- Purchase fee: **$6 CAD**
- Minimum load: **$10 CAD**

2. **How to Use the Presto Card**

Once you've loaded money onto your Presto card, using it is simple. For buses and streetcars, just tap your card on the green reader near the doors when you board. For the subway, tap it at the entrance gates.

Each time you tap, **$3.35 CAD** is deducted from your card for a single ride. If you transfer from a bus to a streetcar or a subway, or between any combination of TTC vehicles, you don't have to pay again as long as you complete your journey within two hours of your first tap. This means you can hop off a streetcar to grab a coffee and get back on without paying extra, as long as it's within the two-hour window.

Pro Tip: Always tap your Presto card when transferring vehicles. The system automatically recognizes that you're within the two-hour transfer window and won't charge you again.

3. **Benefits of Using Presto**

- **Cost savings:** The Presto card fare is slightly cheaper than paying cash. At **$3.35 CAD** per ride compared to **$3.25 CAD** in cash, the savings might seem small, but it adds up over multiple trips.
- **Convenience:** No need to carry cash or tokens. Just tap and go, which is especially handy if you're hopping between buses, streetcars, and subways throughout the day.
- **Transfers:** The two-hour transfer window lets you switch between buses, streetcars, and subways without paying extra, as long as you complete your journey in that time.

Maximizing Savings with Fare Passes

If you plan on using public transit frequently during your stay, TTC offers several passes that can help you save even more.

1. Day Pass

If you're planning on taking multiple TTC trips in a single day, consider purchasing a **Day Pass**. For **$13.50 CAD**, you can ride the TTC as much as you want for the entire day. This is a great deal if you're planning to visit several attractions in one day and will be hopping on and off public transit throughout.

Where to buy: You can load a Day Pass onto your Presto card at TTC vending machines, **Shoppers Drug Mart**, or online. Once you've loaded the pass, just tap your card as usual when boarding, and you'll be able to travel all day without paying extra.

Cost: Day Pass: $13.50 CAD

Pro Tip: If you're planning to explore several neighborhoods like **Kensington Market**, **The Beaches**, and **Distillery District** in a single day, the Day Pass will pay for itself after just four trips.

2. Weekly Pass

For travelers staying in Toronto for more than a few days, the **Weekly Pass** is another great option. It costs **$43.75 CAD** and allows unlimited travel on the TTC for seven consecutive days. This pass is perfect if you're planning a full week of sightseeing or need to use public transit daily for commuting.

Where to buy: Like the Day Pass, you can load a Weekly Pass onto your Presto card.

Cost: Weekly Pass: $43.75 CAD

Pro Tip: If you plan to use public transit twice or more every day for seven days, the Weekly Pass is the best way to save money.

TTC and Accessibility

The TTC is committed to making its public transit system accessible for all travelers. Most TTC buses are low-floor and have ramps that can be lowered to street level for people with mobility devices. Streetcars and subway stations are also equipped with elevators and ramps for easier access.

If you're using a mobility device, simply let the driver know when boarding a bus or streetcar, and they'll assist you. The subway stations with elevators are clearly marked, and TTC staff are available to help.

For more information on accessible travel, you can visit the TTC's website or ask for assistance at any TTC station.

Where the TTC Can Take You

The TTC can take you just about anywhere in Toronto, from tourist hotspots to lesser-known neighborhoods. Here are some popular destinations that are easy to reach on public transit:

- **CN Tower and Ripley's Aquarium:** Take Line 1 to **Union Station** and walk west along Front Street.
- **Distillery District:** Take the 504 King Streetcar to **Distillery Loop**.
- **Royal Ontario Museum:** Take Line 1 to **Museum Station**.
- **High Park:** Take Line 2 to **High Park Station**.
- **Toronto Islands:** Take Line 1 to **Union Station**, then walk to the **Jack Layton Ferry Terminal**.

Exploring Toronto by Foot: Walking-Friendly Routes

1. Downtown Toronto (Union Station to Harbourfront)

Start your walk at **Union Station** (65 Front St W, Toronto, ON M5J 1E6), one of Toronto's architectural gems. It's not just a transit hub; it's a historical building with impressive design. From here, you can walk south towards the **Harbourfront**, passing by several of Toronto's top attractions.

- **Walk down Front Street** and you'll soon see the **CN Tower** (301 Front St W, Toronto, ON M5V 2T6), the city's iconic structure. You don't need to pay to go up if you're on a tight budget; just walking around the tower and taking in the views is enough.
- Continue towards the **Rogers Centre** (1 Blue Jays Way, Toronto, ON M5V 1J1), where you can check out the stadium where the Toronto Blue Jays play.
- From here, head south to **Harbourfront Centre** (235 Queens Quay W, Toronto, ON M5J 2G8). Walking along the lakeshore, you'll enjoy beautiful views of **Lake Ontario**. In the summer, there are often free outdoor performances and art exhibits. There are also places to sit and relax without spending a dime.

This route is packed with sights and is all within walking distance, saving you from having to spend on transport.

2. Kensington Market and Chinatown

One of the best areas to explore by foot is **Kensington Market** (Spadina Ave & Dundas St W, Toronto, ON M5T 2E9). It's a vibrant, multicultural neighborhood filled with colorful street art, vintage shops, and affordable eats. Walking through Kensington feels like you've stepped into a different world, and it won't cost you a thing to take it all in.

- Start at **Spadina Avenue** and make your way through the market's narrow streets. You'll pass small stalls selling everything from handmade goods to international food. If you get hungry, grab a bite at **Seven Lives Tacos** (69 Kensington Ave), where you can get filling tacos for about **$7-10 CAD**.
- After Kensington, head south to **Chinatown** along **Dundas Street West**. Here, you can visit the many affordable Asian markets and shops, or just enjoy the lively atmosphere.

Kensington Market and Chinatown are perfect for budget travelers who want to experience Toronto's local culture without spending a lot. It's easy to walk around these neighborhoods, and you'll find plenty to explore.

3. Distillery District

The **Distillery District** (55 Mill St, Toronto, ON M5A 3C4) is one of Toronto's most charming pedestrian areas. This historic district is full of red-brick buildings, cobblestone streets, and art galleries. Best of all, it's completely walkable.

- Stroll around and enjoy the architecture of the old distillery buildings. The area is often home to free public art installations and street performances.
- If you want to grab a bite, keep an eye out for affordable spots like **Cluny Bistro** (35 Tank House Lane, Toronto), where you can enjoy a pastry for around **$5 CAD**.

Since cars aren't allowed in the district, it's the perfect place to walk around, take photos, and enjoy a peaceful day without having to spend on transportation.

4. Toronto Islands

For a scenic escape from the city, take a ferry to the **Toronto Islands**. The ferry ride itself is affordable, costing **$8.70 CAD** round trip for adults, and once you're on the islands, walking is the best way to get around.

- Start at **Centre Island** and head to the **Centre Island Beach**, one of the nicest beaches in Toronto. You can swim, relax, or walk along the waterfront for stunning views of the city skyline.
- If you want to explore further, you can walk across the islands to **Hanlan's Point** or **Ward's Island**, both peaceful areas with beautiful natural scenery.

The islands offer a perfect walking route, and since most of the activities here are free, it's a great budget-friendly way to spend a day.

5. Queen Street West

Queen Street West is one of Toronto's trendiest neighborhoods, filled with boutique shops, cafes, and street art. It's the kind of place where you can spend hours walking, exploring different shops, and watching street performers, all without having to pay for entry.

- Start at **Bathurst Street** and head west along Queen. You'll pass art galleries, quirky shops, and some great coffee spots like **Jimmy's Coffee** (107 Portland St), where a coffee will cost you around **$3-5 CAD**.
- Don't miss **Graffiti Alley** (between Portland and Spadina), a long alleyway filled with colorful street art. It's free to explore, and you'll get some great photos.

Queen Street West is a great place to explore if you're into art and culture.

GETTING AROUND TORONTO

Walking is the best way to experience it, and it's all very budge

Budget Tips for Taxis, Rideshares, and Bike Rentals

1. **Taxis**

Taxis in Toronto are convenient, but they're also the most expensive option for getting around. A typical taxi ride downtown will cost you anywhere between **$10-20 CAD** depending on the distance and traffic. However, they are good for situations when you're carrying heavy luggage, or when public transit is not running (like late at night).

- **Budget Tip:** Avoid taxis if possible, especially for short distances, as the costs can add up quickly. If you must take a taxi, use it for trips where walking or public transit is not practical. Also, check with your accommodation if they have any partnerships with taxi companies for discounted rates.

Taxi Companies:

- **Beck Taxi:** +1 416-751-5555
- **Diamond Taxi:** +1 416-366-6868

2. **Rideshares (Uber, Lyft)**

Rideshares like **Uber** and **Lyft** are cheaper than taxis but can still be expensive during surge times or high-demand periods. A ride within the downtown area can range from **$10-15 CAD** under normal conditions, but during rush hour or bad weather, prices can increase significantly.

- **Budget Tip:** If you're traveling with a group, rideshares can be cost-effective since you can split the fare. Always check the fare estimate before confirming a ride to avoid surprises. You can also opt for the

Uber Pool or **Lyft Shared** options, which allow you to share your ride with other passengers to reduce costs.

Uber Contact: Uber App
Lyft Contact: Lyft App

3. **Bike Rentals and Bike Share Toronto**

For a more budget-friendly and eco-friendly way to get around, **bike rentals** and **Bike Share Toronto** are great options. Toronto is becoming more bike-friendly with dedicated bike lanes on major streets, and you can easily rent bikes throughout the city.

- **Bike Share Toronto** has stations all over the city, and it's an affordable way to rent a bike. A single ride costs **$3.25 CAD** for 30 minutes, while a day pass (which gives you unlimited 30-minute rides) is **$7 CAD**. You can also get a monthly pass for **$25 CAD** if you're staying longer.
- If you go over the 30-minute ride time, additional charges apply, but you can avoid this by docking your bike at any station before the 30-minute mark and picking up another one.
- **Budget Tip:** Use Bike Share Toronto if you're planning to explore neighborhoods that are slightly further apart, like **Kensington Market** and **Queen Street West**, or if you want to take a scenic ride along the **Toronto Waterfront Trail**. It's an affordable alternative to taxis or rideshares, especially if you like cycling.

Bike Share Toronto:
Bike Share Toronto Website
Customer Service: +1 855-898-2378

If you prefer renting a bike for longer periods, several bike rental shops offer reasonable rates:

- **Wheel Excitement (249 Queens Quay W):** Around **$10 CAD/hour**

or **$35 CAD/day** for standard bikes.
- **Bikes On Wheels (309 Augusta Ave)**: Similar rates for full-day rentals, and they're located near Kensington Market.

Affordable Accommodations

Best Budget Hotels in Toronto

When it comes to budget hotels, Toronto has plenty of options that provide a clean, comfortable stay at reasonable prices. These hotels are ideal for travelers who want private rooms with basic amenities without the hefty price tag of luxury hotels.

1. The Rex Hotel

- **Address:** 194 Queen St W, Toronto, ON M5V 1Z1
- **Cost:** Rooms start at **$130 CAD/night**
- **Contact:** +1 416-598-2475
- **Website:** therex.ca

The Rex is a favorite among budget travelers due to its prime location right on **Queen Street West**. It's a simple hotel, but it's clean, comfortable, and full of character. Rooms are basic but cozy, with private bathrooms, air conditioning, and free Wi-Fi. What makes The Rex stand out is that it's also a jazz bar, so if you love live music, you'll be staying in the heart of it.

It's close to many of Toronto's top attractions, like **Nathan Phillips Square** and the **Art Gallery of Ontario**. The location is great for those who want to explore downtown on foot or by public transit, as streetcars pass right outside the hotel. The cost is very reasonable for the area, and you're not sacrificing comfort for savings.

2. Hotel Ocho

- **Address:** 195 Spadina Ave, Toronto, ON M5T 2C3
- **Cost:** Rooms start at **$150 CAD/night**
- **Contact:** +1 416-593-0885
- **Website:** hotelocho.com

Located near **Chinatown** and **Kensington Market**, Hotel Ocho is a stylish boutique hotel that offers a great balance of comfort and affordability. The rooms are modern with minimalistic decor, hardwood floors, and large windows that give a bright, airy feel. The hotel itself is in a historic building, but the interior is sleek and modern.

Hotel Ocho is a perfect base for exploring the artsy side of Toronto, and it's just a short walk to **Queen Street West** for shopping and dining. While it's on the pricier side for budget travelers, the comfort and style make it worth the slightly higher price. Plus, you're in one of Toronto's trendiest areas.

3. The Alexandra Hotel

- **Address:** 77 Ryerson Ave, Toronto, ON M5T 2V4
- **Cost:** Rooms start at **$120 CAD/night**
- **Contact:** +1 416-504-2121
- **Website:** alexandrahotel.com

The Alexandra Hotel is one of the more affordable options in the heart of downtown Toronto. It's located near **Kensington Market** and **Queen Street West**, making it easy to explore these popular neighborhoods without spending on transportation. The hotel is simple, offering basic amenities like kitchenettes in each room, free Wi-Fi, and private bathrooms.

It's not a luxury experience, but it's clean and quiet, perfect for travelers who want a no-frills stay in a central location. The kitchenette is a big plus if you're trying to save money by preparing your own meals. Overall, it's a great choice for budget travelers who want to be close to Toronto's action without paying high downtown prices.

4. The Neill-Wycik Hotel

- **Address:** 96 Gerrard St E, Toronto, ON M5B 1G7
- **Cost:** Rooms start at **$70 CAD/night** (seasonal availability, May-September)
- **Contact:** +1 416-977-2320
- **Website:** neill-wycik.com

The Neill-Wycik Hotel is actually a student residence that operates as a budget hotel during the summer months. If you're visiting Toronto between May and September, this is one of the cheapest places to stay in the city. The rooms are dorm-style, with shared bathrooms and kitchens, but they're clean and functional.

It's located near **Ryerson University**, which means it's right in the heart of downtown. You're a short walk from the **Eaton Centre**, **Yonge-Dundas Square**, and **Nathan Phillips Square**. It's perfect for budget travelers who don't mind a more basic stay in exchange for prime location and incredibly low prices.

Hostels for Solo Travelers and Backpackers

1. HI Toronto Hostel (Hostelling International)

- **Address:** 76 Church St, Toronto, ON M5C 2G1

AFFORDABLE ACCOMMODATIONS

- **Cost:** Dorms start at **$40 CAD/night**, private rooms start at **$80 CAD/night**
- **Contact:** +1 416-971-4440
- **Website:** hihostels.ca

HI Toronto Hostel is one of the best-known hostels in the city and for good reason. It's located right in the downtown core, making it easy to walk to many of Toronto's attractions, like the **St. Lawrence Market** and **The Distillery District**. This hostel is popular with solo travelers and backpackers because it offers a great social environment, including events like pub crawls and walking tours.

The dorms are clean and well-maintained, with lockers for your valuables. If you prefer more privacy, they also have private rooms available at a slightly higher cost. There's a shared kitchen, so you can save money by cooking your own meals, and breakfast is included in the price. This is one of the best hostels for travelers who want to meet people and enjoy a central location.

2. Planet Traveler Hostel

- **Address:** 357 College St, Toronto, ON M5T 1S5
- **Cost:** Dorms start at **$40 CAD/night**, private rooms start at **$100 CAD/night**
- **Contact:** +1 647-352-8747
- **Website:** theplanettraveler.com

Planet Traveler Hostel is located in the heart of **Kensington Market**, one of Toronto's coolest neighborhoods. It's a very eco-friendly hostel, with solar panels and energy-efficient systems, making it a great choice for environmentally conscious travelers. The hostel has a relaxed vibe, with a rooftop patio that offers stunning views of the Toronto skyline.

The dorms are spacious and clean, with individual power outlets and lights for each bed. Private rooms are also available for those who prefer a bit more privacy. This hostel has a very social atmosphere, with a communal kitchen, movie nights, and free breakfast. It's perfect for solo travelers who want to meet others in a laid-back setting while still being close to major attractions like **Chinatown** and **Little Italy**.

3. The Only Backpacker's Inn

- **Address:** 972 Danforth Ave, Toronto, ON M4J 1L9
- **Cost:** Dorms start at **$35 CAD/night**, private rooms start at **$85 CAD/night**
- **Contact:** +1 416-463-3249
- **Website:** theonlyinn.com

If you're looking for something a little different, The Only Backpacker's Inn is located in **The Danforth** (also known as **Greektown**), a bit outside the downtown core but in a lively, local neighborhood. It's close to the **Danforth subway station**, so getting downtown is easy, and it's also a great place to experience Toronto's diverse food scene.

This hostel has a welcoming, homey vibe, with a bar downstairs where guests can mingle. The dorms are clean and simple, and private rooms are available for those who want a quieter stay. Free breakfast is included, and there's a fully equipped kitchen if you want to cook your own meals. The atmosphere here is a bit more laid-back than some of the downtown hostels, making it a good choice for solo travelers who prefer a quieter environment while still being able to meet others.

4. Two Peas Pod Hostel

- **Address:** 403 Spadina Ave, Toronto, ON M5T 2G6
- **Cost:** Dorms start at **$45 CAD/night**
- **Contact:** +1 416-792-3500

- **Website:** twopeaspodhostel.com

Two Peas Pod Hostel is located on **Spadina Avenue**, close to **Kensington Market** and **Chinatown**. This hostel offers a modern, clean environment with pod-style beds in the dorms, providing a bit more privacy than the typical bunk bed setup. Each pod comes with a curtain, power outlet, and light, which is perfect for solo travelers who want a bit of personal space even in a shared dorm.

There's a rooftop terrace with great views of the city, and the hostel offers free breakfast each morning. While it's slightly more expensive than some other hostels, the modern facilities and privacy make it a great option for those who want to stay in a hostel without sacrificing comfort.

Short-Term Rentals and Airbnb: How to Find Affordable Stays

Short-term rentals like those found on **Airbnb** and similar platforms are an excellent option for budget travelers looking for a more flexible, home-like environment during their stay. With the ability to rent entire apartments, private rooms, or shared spaces, there are options for all types of travelers.

1. **How to Use Airbnb for Affordable Stays**

Airbnb offers a wide variety of accommodation options, from private rooms in someone's apartment to full apartments or houses. To get the best deals, here are a few tips:

- **Book Early:** The earlier you book, the better the chance of finding an affordable place, especially if you're planning to visit during peak times (like summer or during major events like the Toronto International Film Festival). Waiting until the last minute can lead to higher prices, especially in popular areas like downtown Toronto, **Queen Street West**, or **Kensington Market**.

- **Look for Long-Stay Discounts:** Many Airbnb hosts offer discounts for longer stays. If you're planning to stay in Toronto for a week or more, you can often find discounts ranging from **10% to 25%** off the total cost. You'll find these options listed under "Monthly Stays" on Airbnb, which could significantly reduce the cost if you're staying longer.
- **Consider Staying Outside Downtown:** While downtown Toronto has many attractions, accommodations here are generally more expensive. Consider looking for places in neighborhoods like **Parkdale**, **The Junction**, or **Danforth**. These areas are well-connected by public transit (TTC), but tend to be more affordable. A short-term rental in these neighborhoods could cost **$50-80 CAD** per night for a private room, compared to **$100-150 CAD** for something similar in the downtown core.
- **Filter by Price:** Use Airbnb's filtering options to set your price range. Be realistic about your budget and filter for stays that fall within it. Prices can range from **$40 CAD per night** for a shared space to **$120 CAD per night** for an entire apartment, so use these filters to avoid wasting time on listings that are out of your price range.
- **Read Reviews Carefully:** Look for listings with good reviews and ratings. It's not just about finding a cheap place; you want to make sure the host is reliable and the place is clean. Don't be tempted by listings with no reviews, even if the price seems too good to be true—it often is.
- **Avoid Extra Fees:** Some Airbnb listings come with additional cleaning fees or service fees that can add a significant amount to your total. Always check the final price, which includes taxes and fees, before booking. Some hosts charge minimal or no extra fees, which can make a big difference on a budget.

2. Other Platforms for Short-Term Rentals

While Airbnb is the most popular option, there are other platforms you can use to find affordable short-term rentals in Toronto.

- **Vrbo:** Similar to Airbnb, but more focused on full apartment or house rentals, making it a good option if you're traveling with family or a group of friends. Prices here are comparable to Airbnb, but sometimes you can find better deals for larger properties.
- **Booking.com:** While known for hotels, Booking.com also has listings for short-term apartments and vacation rentals. Keep an eye out for "Genius" discounts, which offer additional savings for frequent users.
- **Homestay.com:** This platform allows you to rent a room in someone's home, often at lower prices than Airbnb. It's a great way to save money while getting a more local experience.

Tip: Always compare prices across platforms before booking. Sometimes, the same listing can be cheaper on one platform than another due to different service fees or discount programs.

3. **Areas to Look For Short-Term Rentals in Toronto**

- **Kensington Market (Spadina Ave & Dundas St W):** Known for its artsy vibe and proximity to Chinatown, Kensington Market offers affordable short-term rentals. Expect to pay around **$70-100 CAD** per night for a private room.
- **The Annex (Bloor St W & Spadina Ave):** A lively neighborhood near the University of Toronto. Rentals here are slightly more expensive but still affordable compared to downtown. A private room can go for **$80-120 CAD** per night.
- **Danforth (Broadview Ave & Danforth Ave):** Also known as Greektown, Danforth is slightly further from downtown but very affordable. You can find entire apartments here for around **$80-110 CAD** per night.

Contacts for Airbnb Toronto Support:
Airbnb Customer Support: Airbnb Help
Vrbo Customer Support: Vrbo Support

University Dorms and Summer Housing Options

During the summer, when students are away, several universities in Toronto open their dorms to travelers. This is a fantastic option for budget-conscious travelers looking for simple, affordable accommodations. University dorms are typically centrally located and offer basic amenities like Wi-Fi, shared bathrooms, and common areas. They're not luxurious, but they're clean, convenient, and affordable.

1. **University of Toronto Dorms**

The **University of Toronto** (St. George Campus) is one of the largest universities in the city and offers dorm accommodations during the summer months (typically from May to August).

- **Types of Rooms:** You can choose from single rooms, double rooms, and even apartment-style accommodations depending on the residence. Most dorms offer shared bathrooms, but some apartment-style options come with private bathrooms and kitchenettes.
- **Cost:** Prices for dorms at U of T range from **$50-90 CAD per night** for a single or double room. This is a great deal considering the location, which is right in the heart of downtown Toronto, close to **Queen's Park** and **Bloor Street**.
- **How to Book:** You can book a room through the University of Toronto's summer accommodation website. It's recommended to book early, as rooms tend to fill up quickly, especially in June and July when events like **Pride Toronto** and the **Toronto Jazz Festival** attract more visitors.

Contact Information:
University of Toronto Summer Residence
Address: 89 Chestnut St, Toronto, ON M5G 1R1
Phone: +1 416-585-3000
Website: U of T Summer Residences

2. Ryerson University Dorms

Ryerson University (soon to be renamed **Toronto Metropolitan University**) also offers summer accommodations for budget travelers. Located near **Yonge-Dundas Square**, it's ideal for travelers who want to be close to shopping, restaurants, and attractions like the **Eaton Centre**.

- **Types of Rooms:** Ryerson offers private rooms with shared or private bathrooms. Some dorms have air conditioning and laundry facilities, which are a bonus during the summer heat.
- **Cost:** Expect to pay around **$60-80 CAD per night** for a private room with shared bathroom facilities. Larger suites with private bathrooms and kitchenettes cost a bit more but are still affordable compared to hotels in the area.
- **How to Book:** You can book directly through Ryerson's summer housing website. Be sure to check for any student discount rates if you're a student, as some universities offer lower prices for students, even if they're not attending that particular university.

Contact Information:
Ryerson University Summer Residence
Address: 160 Mutual St, Toronto, ON M5B 2M2
Phone: +1 416-979-5000
Website: Ryerson University Summer Housing

3. York University Dorms

Located a bit further north from downtown, **York University** also offers budget-friendly summer accommodations. While it's not as central as U of T or Ryerson, it's still well-connected by public transit (subway Line 1).

- **Types of Rooms:** York offers a range of accommodations, from single dorm rooms to suite-style units with private kitchens and bathrooms.
- **Cost:** Prices are similar to other universities, ranging from **$50-75 CAD**

per night. It's a great option if you don't mind being a bit further from the downtown core.
- **How to Book:** You can book through York's website. As with other universities, it's a good idea to book early, especially if you're visiting during busy times like **Caribana** or the **Canadian National Exhibition (CNE)**.

Contact Information:
York University Housing
Address: 4700 Keele St, Toronto, ON M3J 1P3
Phone: +1 416-736-5000
Website: York University Housing

Tips for Booking University Dorms

- **Book Early:** As with any budget accommodation, university dorms fill up fast, especially during peak summer months. Try to book at least 2-3 months in advance to secure your spot.
- **Check for Discounts:** Some universities offer discounts for long-term stays (a week or more) or for students from other universities. It's worth asking about these discounts when you book.
- **Be Prepared for Basic Amenities:** While university dorms are clean and safe, they are fairly basic. Don't expect luxury amenities. Bring your own toiletries and be prepared to share bathrooms in most cases.

Tips for Getting Last-Minute Accommodation Deals

1. Use Last-Minute Booking Apps and Websites

Several apps and websites are specifically designed to help travelers find last-minute accommodation deals. These platforms offer discounted rooms that hotels and other properties are looking to fill quickly. They work well for budget travelers who don't mind waiting until the last minute to secure a room. Here are some of the best ones to use:

HotelTonight

- **HotelTonight** is one of the most popular apps for finding last-minute hotel rooms. It specializes in unsold rooms, offering deep discounts—often up to 50% off. The app is easy to use and allows you to book a room for the same night or up to a week in advance. The great thing about HotelTonight is that it only shows rooms that are immediately available, and it highlights budget options along with more upscale choices.
- **Risks and rewards:** While you can score a great deal, availability might be limited, especially during busy times like holidays or festivals. It's best to use this app when you have some flexibility.
- **Download:** HotelTonight App
- **Cost:** Rooms on HotelTonight can start as low as **$70 CAD** in downtown Toronto, but average around **$120-150 CAD** depending on the time of year.

Booking.com

- **Booking.com** is one of the most reliable platforms for finding last-minute deals. They offer everything from hostels and budget hotels to high-end properties, and they frequently run last-minute promotions. The **"Book Now, Pay Later"** option allows you to reserve a room without paying upfront, which gives you some flexibility to change

your plans if needed.
- **Risks and rewards:** Booking late can sometimes mean you don't get your first choice, especially if you're looking in a popular area like downtown Toronto. But you might find a room that was discounted last-minute.
- **Website:** Booking.com
- **Cost:** You can find hostel beds starting at **$40-50 CAD** per night, while budget hotels might go for **$80-120 CAD**.

Hotwire

Hotwire is known for its **"Hot Rate"** deals, which can save you up to 60% on hotels. The catch is that you won't know the exact name of the hotel until after you've booked it. However, the website does provide information on the hotel's star rating, amenities, and approximate location, so you can make an educated guess about where you'll be staying.

- **Risks and rewards:** This is a great option if you don't mind a bit of mystery. If you're okay with taking a chance on where exactly you'll stay, you could score a very nice room at a heavily discounted rate.
- **Website:** Hotwire.com
- **Cost:** With Hotwire's "Hot Rate" deals, rooms in Toronto can range from **$80-150 CAD** for a 3-star hotel in a central location.

Expedia

- **Expedia** often offers last-minute deals through its **mobile app**, where you can find discounted hotels, flights, and vacation packages. The app is user-friendly, and like Booking.com, it has a **"Pay Later"** feature for hotels. Expedia also has a rewards program, so if you use it often, you can collect points to save on future bookings.
- **Risks and rewards:** Expedia is great for booking entire vacation

packages at the last minute. However, during peak travel seasons, the best rooms can be booked up quickly, so your choices might be limited.
- **Website:** Expedia.com
- **Cost:** Rooms start at **$60-100 CAD** for budget hotels, with higher-end hotels averaging **$130-200 CAD** depending on the location.

Priceline

- **Priceline** has a **"Name Your Own Price"** feature where you can bid on hotel rooms. You set your budget, and Priceline tries to match you with a hotel that's willing to accept your offer. If the bid goes through, you get the room at your price. The downside is that this feature is no longer as widely available as it used to be, but when it works, it can result in major savings.
- **Risks and rewards:** The main risk is that your bid might not be accepted, which means you'll have to try again or book at the regular price. However, it's worth it if you're feeling flexible and want to save as much as possible.
- **Website:** Priceline.com
- **Cost:** Rooms in Toronto through Priceline can range from **$60-120 CAD**, depending on the bid and availability.

2. Look for Deals on Hotel Websites

Sometimes the best last-minute deals aren't on third-party apps but directly on the hotel's own website. Many hotels offer special promotions, such as **"Stay 3 nights, get the 4th night free"** or discounts for booking within a few days of your stay. Checking directly can also help you avoid booking fees, which are often included when you go through an intermediary site.

- **Budget Tip:** Always sign up for a hotel's rewards program or email

list. Hotels frequently send out last-minute deals to their subscribers. Hotels like the **Holiday Inn Toronto Downtown Centre** (30 Carlton St, Toronto, ON M5B 2E9) or **The Rex Hotel** (194 Queen St W, Toronto, ON M5V 1Z1) often run promotions for members.
- **Cost:** Rooms at places like **The Rex Hotel** can go for **$100-150 CAD** on a last-minute deal, while more budget-friendly chains like **Holiday Inn** offer rooms starting around **$120 CAD** per night.

3. **Hostel and Short-Term Rental Deals**

For budget travelers, hostels and short-term rentals like **Airbnb** or **Vrbo** can offer great last-minute options. Many of these properties drop their prices when they have empty rooms close to the booking date. However, hostels tend to fill up quickly during peak season, so be prepared to move fast if you see a deal.

Hostelworld: One of the best platforms for booking hostels is **Hostelworld**. They offer last-minute deals, and because Toronto has a few excellent hostels, you might find a great spot at a low cost. For example, **Planet Traveler Hostel** (357 College St, Toronto, ON M5T 1S5) is one of the top-rated hostels in the city, offering dorm beds for around **$40-50 CAD** per night, and it's close to Kensington Market.

- **Risks and rewards:** Hostels are usually cheap and cheerful, but they fill up fast, so availability might be limited if you're booking late. The reward, however, is a great price for a central location.
- **Airbnb:** If you're looking for something more private than a hostel, **Airbnb** often has last-minute rental deals. If a host has an empty calendar, they're likely to lower the nightly rate to attract last-minute bookings. However, Airbnb prices can still fluctuate based on demand, so you'll want to compare it to hotel options.
- **Risks and rewards:** The main risk is that last-minute Airbnbs might still be pricier than budget hotels or hostels, especially in downtown

Toronto. However, if you're flexible about staying outside the core, you might find cheaper options.
- **Cost:** Rooms on Airbnb in Toronto can range from **$70-150 CAD** per night depending on the location and type of accommodation.

4. Loyalty Programs and Membership Discounts

If you're part of any loyalty programs or have memberships with organizations like **AAA** or **CAA**, you can often use these for last-minute hotel discounts. Many budget hotels in Toronto, including chains like **Comfort Inn** or **Days Inn**, offer special rates for members.

- **Budget Tip:** Even if you're booking last-minute, check if the hotel offers discounts for **AAA**, **CAA**, or other associations. You could save up to **10-15%** on your room rate, which is a nice bonus for budget travelers.

Comfort Inn Toronto City Centre
Address: 321 Jarvis St, Toronto, ON M5B 2C2
Contact: +1 416-368-1990
Cost: Rates typically start at **$100-140 CAD** per night for last-minute bookings, with discounts available for loyalty members.

5. What to Keep in Mind When Booking Last-Minute

While booking late can result in great deals, there are a few things to keep in mind to make sure you're not caught off guard:

- **Limited Options:** The closer you get to your travel date, the fewer options you'll have. This is especially true during peak times, like holidays, festivals, or busy weekends. If you're set on staying in a specific neighborhood, be prepared that your first choice might not be available.
- **Higher Prices in Peak Season:** During high-demand periods (like **Toronto International Film Festival** in September or summer week-

ends), prices can still be higher even last-minute. Always compare rates to see if you're truly getting a deal.
- **Cancellation Policies:** Some last-minute deals are non-refundable, meaning once you book, you're locked in. Always check the cancellation policy before confirming to avoid losing money if your plans change unexpectedly.
- **Safety Considerations:** If you're booking through lesser-known platforms or private short-term rentals, make sure to read reviews and verify the host's profile. Staying in a well-reviewed hostel or hotel is usually safer for budget travelers.

Dining on a Budget

Cheap Eats in Toronto: Neighborhoods with Affordable Food

Toronto's diverse neighborhoods offer a range of cuisine at prices that fit any budget. Whether you're craving Chinese dumplings, Mexican tacos, or Middle Eastern shawarma, these areas are packed with affordable spots to grab a meal.

1. Chinatown

Chinatown, centered around **Spadina Avenue** and **Dundas Street West**, is one of the best places in Toronto for affordable Asian cuisine. Here, you can find everything from steaming bowls of pho to dumplings and stir-fried noodles, all at budget-friendly prices.

- **Pho Hung** (350 Spadina Ave) is a favorite spot for a large bowl of Vietnamese pho, perfect for warming up on a chilly day. A large bowl costs around **$10-12 CAD**, and it's filling enough that you won't need anything else.
- **Mother's Dumplings** (421 Spadina Ave) serves up some of the best handmade dumplings in the city. You can get a plate of 12 dumplings for about **$8-10 CAD**, depending on your filling choice (pork, shrimp, or vegetarian).
- If you're looking for something quick, check out the **New Sky Restaurant** (353 Spadina Ave) for classic Chinese dishes like fried rice, stir-fried

vegetables, and noodle soups, with prices starting around **$7-9 CAD** for smaller dishes.

Chinatown is a great place to fill up without emptying your wallet, and it's easy to find vegetarian and vegan options here as well.

2. Kensington Market

Just around the corner from Chinatown is **Kensington Market**, one of Toronto's most vibrant and diverse neighborhoods. Here, you'll find food from all over the world, and the best part is that most meals are priced with budget travelers in mind.

- **Seven Lives Tacos** (69 Kensington Ave) is famous for its Baja-style tacos, and for good reason. A taco here will set you back around **$7-9 CAD**, and one is often enough to satisfy, especially if you get the **Gobernador** (a shrimp and cheese taco).
- For something sweet, stop by **Pancho's Bakery** (214 Augusta Ave) for their **churros**. At around **$4 CAD** for a piping hot churro filled with dulce de leche, it's a cheap but satisfying treat.
- If you're into Caribbean flavors, try **Rasta Pasta** (61 Kensington Ave), a mix of Jamaican and Italian cuisine. You can get a jerk chicken sandwich for about **$6-8 CAD**, making it one of the best value meals in the area.

Kensington Market is perfect for walking around and grabbing a snack or meal on the go. You'll find everything from Mexican to Caribbean to Middle Eastern food, and most of it is very affordable.

3. Little India

If you're craving Indian food, head over to **Gerrard Street East** between **Coxwell Avenue** and **Greenwood Avenue**, known as **Little India**. This area is packed with restaurants offering flavorful curries, biryanis, and tandoori dishes at reasonable prices.

- **Lahore Tikka House** (1365 Gerrard St E) is one of the most popular spots, where you can get a large plate of chicken tikka, naan, and rice for around **$12-15 CAD**. The portions are big enough to share if you're not too hungry.
- For something even cheaper, try **Motimahal Restaurant** (1422 Gerrard St E), where a meal of butter chicken and rice will cost you about **$10 CAD**. The restaurant may not look fancy, but the food is authentic and satisfying.

Little India is one of the best places to get a filling meal for under **$15 CAD**, and the variety of vegetarian dishes here is excellent.

4. Greektown (Danforth Avenue)

Greektown, along **Danforth Avenue**, is famous for its authentic Greek cuisine, but you can find lots of budget-friendly Mediterranean food as well.

- **Messini Authentic Gyros** (445 Danforth Ave) is a popular spot for gyros, souvlaki, and other Greek fast food. A gyro sandwich stuffed with meat, tzatziki, and vegetables will only set you back around **$6-8 CAD**, and it's big enough to keep you full for hours.
- **Astoria Shish Kebob House** (390 Danforth Ave) offers more traditional Greek meals, with souvlaki platters starting around **$12 CAD**. You get a full plate with salad, potatoes, rice, and pita bread, which makes it a great deal for the price.

Greektown is not only known for its food but also for its friendly vibe. You can walk down Danforth Avenue and find cheap eats at almost every corner.

Best Street Food and Food Trucks: Quick and Budget-Friendly Meals

1. The Blue Donkey Streatery

One of the best food trucks in Toronto is **The Blue Donkey Streatery**, known for its Greek street food. You can find them at various locations around the city, especially during food truck festivals and events.

- Their **Greek poutine**, which is fries topped with feta, gravy, and meat, costs about **$10 CAD** and is hearty enough for a full meal.
- For something lighter, their **chicken souvlaki wrap** is only **$8 CAD** and is packed with flavor.

Location: Various locations around Toronto, check their social media for updates.

2. Buster's Sea Cove

If you're in the mood for seafood, **Buster's Sea Cove** is one of the most popular seafood trucks in the city. You can also find their permanent location at **St. Lawrence Market** (93 Front St E), but their food truck is often spotted downtown.

- A lobster roll from Buster's will cost you around **$14 CAD**, and though it's a bit pricier for street food, it's packed with fresh lobster and worth every penny.
- For something cheaper, try their **fish tacos** for about **$9 CAD**, which are crispy and flavorful.

Location: Downtown Toronto, near food truck hotspots like **Nathan Phillips Square**.

3. Fidel Gastro's

For those looking for bold, inventive street food, **Fidel Gastro's** serves up some of the most unique sandwiches in the city. Their food truck, **Priscilla**, moves around Toronto, so check online to find them.

- One of their best sellers is the **Porknado**, a pulled pork sandwich with slaw and hot sauce. It costs about **$10-12 CAD**, and the portion is generous.
- If you're not into pork, their **Buffalo Chicken Mac 'N Cheese** sandwich is another favorite, with prices also starting around **$10 CAD**.

Location: Check their Twitter or Instagram for locations, often seen at festivals and downtown spots.

4. Heirloom Food Truck

If you're looking for vegan or vegetarian street food, the **Heirloom Food Truck** offers plant-based meals that are both healthy and affordable.

- The **BBQ Pulled Jackfruit Sandwich** is one of their top picks, costing about **$9 CAD**. It's a flavorful, vegan alternative to pulled pork.
- They also serve a delicious **vegan poutine**, which costs around **$8-10 CAD** depending on the toppings.

Location: Often found near **Ryerson University** and **Nathan Phillips Square**.

5. Toronto's Hot Dog Carts

You can't talk about street food in Toronto without mentioning the iconic hot dog carts. These carts are stationed all over downtown, especially around **Yonge Street** and **Dundas Square**.

- A basic hot dog or sausage will cost you around **$3-5 CAD**, and you can load it up with a variety of free toppings like onions, pickles, mustard, and ketchup.
- For a little more variety, some carts offer veggie dogs or spicy sausages

for about **$5-6 CAD**.

These carts are perfect for a quick and cheap bite, especially when you're walking around the city.

Top Budget Restaurants: Chinatown, Little Italy, and More

1. Chinatown

Chinatown is one of the best areas to find affordable and authentic Asian cuisine. The restaurants here serve large portions at great prices, making it ideal for budget travelers. You'll find everything from dumplings to pho, all at prices that won't hurt your wallet.

Mother's Dumplings (421 Spadina Ave, Toronto, ON M5T 2G6)
This spot is a favorite for locals and travelers alike. **Mother's Dumplings** serves handmade dumplings, noodles, and soups. A plate of dumplings here will cost you around **$8-12 CAD**, and they're very filling. The vibe is casual, and you can even watch the dumplings being made fresh. It's perfect for lunch or dinner.

Pho Hung (350 Spadina Ave, Toronto, ON M5T 2G4)
For a great bowl of pho, **Pho Hung** is the place to go. Located right on Spadina, this Vietnamese spot serves large bowls of steaming hot pho for **$10-15 CAD**. The portions are generous, so if you're hungry after exploring Chinatown, this is the spot to fill up without overspending.

Swatow Restaurant (309 Spadina Ave, Toronto, ON M5T 2E6)
Swatow is another classic Chinese restaurant in Chinatown known for its fast service and affordable prices. A big bowl of wonton soup will set you back about **$7-10 CAD**, and the stir-fried noodles are delicious and around **$12-15 CAD**. It's no-frills but very popular among locals.

2. Little Italy

Little Italy is famous for its charming streets and authentic Italian cuisine, but you don't have to spend big to eat here. There are plenty of budget-friendly Italian eateries that serve delicious pasta, pizza, and more.

Cafe Diplomatico (594 College St, Toronto, ON M6G 1B3)

Cafe Dip, as it's known locally, has been a neighborhood favorite since the 1960s. It's a casual spot with great pizza, pasta, and sandwiches. You can get a personal pizza for about **$10-12 CAD**, and their pasta dishes start around **$12-15 CAD**. If the weather is nice, grab a seat on the patio and people-watch while enjoying your meal.

Bitondo's Pizzeria (11 Clinton St, Toronto, ON M6J 2N7)

For a quick and cheap slice, head to **Bitondo's**. This classic pizzeria has been serving up some of the best pizza in Little Italy for decades. A large slice of pizza costs around **$3.50 CAD**, and their famous panzerotti (stuffed pizza pockets) are about **$7-8 CAD**. It's the perfect spot for a budget-friendly lunch.

Sotto Voce Wine & Pasta Bar (595 College St, Toronto, ON M6G 1B5)

Though slightly more upscale, **Sotto Voce** offers excellent happy hour deals. From **4-6 PM**, you can get discounted pasta dishes and drinks. Their gnocchi and risotto are fan favorites, and you can expect to pay **$15-20 CAD** during happy hour, making it a great budget option for early dinners.

3. Koreatown

Koreatown, located along **Bloor Street** between **Bathurst and Christie**, is another excellent place for budget dining. Korean cuisine is filling, flavorful, and usually quite affordable.

The Owl of Minerva (700 Bloor St W, Toronto, ON M6G 1L4)

This small, no-frills Korean spot is famous for its **pork bone soup** (Gamjatang), which costs about **$10-12 CAD** and comes with plenty of sides like kimchi and rice. It's a hearty meal that will keep you full for hours without spending much.

Buk Chang Dong Soon Tofu (691 Bloor St W, Toronto, ON M6G 1L3)

Another Koreatown favorite, **Buk Chang Dong Soon Tofu** specializes in soft tofu soup. A bowl of their famous tofu stew costs around **$10-12 CAD**, and it comes with banchan (Korean side dishes) and rice. This place is great for a budget dinner after a day of exploring the city.

4. Greektown

Greektown, along **Danforth Avenue**, is known for its delicious Mediterranean food. While some of the restaurants here can be pricier, there are still plenty of affordable spots to enjoy a great meal on a budget.

Messini Authentic Gyros (445 Danforth Ave, Toronto, ON M4K 1P1)

Messini is a Greektown staple where you can get a huge gyro for just **$7-8 CAD**. Their souvlaki and pita wraps are equally affordable, and the portions are large, so you won't leave hungry. It's one of the best deals in the area for a quick, tasty meal.

Pantheon Restaurant (407 Danforth Ave, Toronto, ON M4K 1P1)

While Pantheon is more of a sit-down restaurant, it offers excellent value for money, especially if you order their lunch specials. You can get a generous plate of grilled meat or seafood with rice, potatoes, and salad for about **$12-15 CAD**. If you want to enjoy Greek food without overspending, it's worth stopping by during lunch hours.

DINING ON A BUDGET

Markets for Cheap Eats: St. Lawrence Market and Kensington Market

1. St. Lawrence Market

Located in the heart of downtown, **St. Lawrence Market** (93 Front St E, Toronto, ON M5E 1C3) is one of Toronto's most famous food markets. It's a great place to find affordable eats, especially if you want to try local specialties.

- **Carousel Bakery**: Known for its famous **peameal bacon sandwich**, a classic Toronto snack. It's filling and costs around **$7-8 CAD**. If you want to taste one of Toronto's signature dishes on a budget, this is the place to go.
- **Buster's Sea Cove**: For seafood lovers, **Buster's** offers fresh seafood at reasonable prices. Their fish and chips cost about **$10-12 CAD**, and the portions are generous. It's perfect if you're looking for something hearty but affordable.
- **Mustachio**: If you're craving Italian, head to **Mustachio** for their famous **eggplant sandwich**, which costs around **$8-10 CAD**. It's a local favorite and big enough to keep you satisfied for lunch.

At **St. Lawrence Market**, you can also find plenty of grocery stalls selling fresh produce, cheese, bread, and other essentials. If you're staying in an Airbnb or a hostel with kitchen access, buying fresh ingredients here can be a cost-effective way to cook your own meals.

Market Hours:
Tuesday to Friday: 9 AM to 5 PM
Saturday: 5 AM to 4 PM
Closed Sunday and Monday.

2. Kensington Market

Kensington Market (Spadina Ave & Dundas St W, Toronto, ON M5T

2E9) is a vibrant, eclectic neighborhood known for its variety of cheap eats. It's a great place to wander around, sample different cuisines, and find affordable meals.

- **Seven Lives Tacos** (69 Kensington Ave, Toronto, ON M5T 2K2): This is the go-to spot for cheap, delicious tacos. You can get one of their famous fish tacos for about **$6-8 CAD**. The portions are big, so one taco might be enough for a light meal. Seven Lives is always busy, but it's worth the wait.
- **Rasta Pasta** (61 Kensington Ave, Toronto, ON M5T 2K1): A mix of Italian and Jamaican cuisine, **Rasta Pasta** is known for its jerk chicken sandwich, which costs around **$7-9 CAD**. It's one of the best cheap eats in Kensington, with bold flavors and large portions.
- **Perola's Supermarket** (247 Augusta Ave, Toronto, ON M5T 2L8): If you're looking for a quick snack, stop by **Perola's**. It's a small Latin American grocery store that also serves fresh empanadas and tamales. These snacks are affordable, costing about **$3-5 CAD** each, and they're perfect for grabbing on the go.

In addition to the food stalls, Kensington Market has several small grocery stores where you can buy fresh produce, bread, and spices. It's an excellent place to pick up ingredients for cooking if you're staying somewhere with kitchen facilities.

Market Hours:

Most vendors are open daily, but the best time to visit is during the day between 10 AM and 6 PM.

DINING ON A BUDGET

Budget-Friendly Vegetarian and Vegan Options

1. Fresh on Spadina

One of the most popular vegetarian and vegan restaurant chains in Toronto is **Fresh**. With several locations throughout the city, the **Fresh on Spadina** location (147 Spadina Ave, Toronto, ON M5V 2L7) is a favorite among locals and travelers alike. The menu is entirely plant-based, offering a range of affordable dishes, from hearty salads to burgers and bowls.

- **Must-try dishes:** The **Quinoa Onion Rings** are a big hit, crispy and full of flavor, priced at around **$7 CAD**. Another favorite is the **BBQ Burger**, made with a house-made veggie patty, lettuce, tomatoes, and smoky BBQ sauce, for around **$15 CAD**. If you're looking for something lighter, the **Big Fresh Bowl**, with mixed greens, brown rice, tofu, and avocado, costs about **$14 CAD**.
- **Why it's budget-friendly:** Fresh offers large portions, making it easy to share dishes or take leftovers. The prices are mid-range for a sit-down restaurant, but you're getting healthy, filling meals with great value for your money.
- **Location:** Fresh on Spadina 147 Spadina Ave, Toronto, ON M5V 2L7
- **Cost:** Main dishes range from **$12-16 CAD**
- **How to get there:** Located near Queen St W, you can easily walk from the Spadina streetcar stop or take a short Uber ride.

2. Hogtown Vegan

For budget-friendly, hearty vegan comfort food, **Hogtown Vegan** (382 College St, Toronto, ON M5T 1S7) is a go-to spot. This restaurant specializes in indulgent vegan dishes that mimic classic comfort food but with a healthy twist. Despite being a sit-down restaurant, the prices are reasonable, and the portion sizes are generous.

- **Must-try dishes:** Their **Unchicken and Waffles** is a standout dish,

priced at **$15 CAD**. It's a crispy, plant-based chicken on top of fluffy waffles with maple syrup—a perfect brunch or dinner meal. For something a little different, try the **Phish and Chips** made with breaded tofu, which goes for about **$14 CAD**.
- **Why it's budget-friendly:** The large portion sizes make Hogtown Vegan an excellent place to stretch your dollar. You can often split a dish or take home leftovers for the next day. Plus, they have frequent specials that can make eating out even cheaper.
- **Location:** Hogtown Vegan 382 College St, Toronto, ON M5T 1S7
- **Cost:** Main dishes range from **$12-15 CAD**
- **How to get there:** It's located in the lively **Kensington Market** area, easily accessible by the College St streetcar.

3. **Kupfert & Kim**

For a quick, affordable, and healthy bite, **Kupfert & Kim** is a popular plant-based, gluten-free eatery with several locations across Toronto. Their **Brookfield Place** location (181 Bay St, Toronto, ON M5J 2T3) is perfect for grabbing a budget-friendly meal if you're exploring downtown or near the Financial District.

- **Must-try dishes:** The **Kim Bowl** is one of their best-sellers, featuring brown rice, sweet potato, greens, chickpeas, and kimchi for **$13 CAD**. Their **Zucchini Noodles** with almond butter sauce and sesame seeds are another light yet filling option, priced around **$11 CAD**.
- **Why it's budget-friendly:** Kupfert & Kim's meals are nutrient-dense, meaning you get a lot of healthy bang for your buck. Plus, most of their bowls and dishes are around **$12-15 CAD**, making them a solid choice for budget-conscious travelers who want to eat clean.
- **Location:** Kupfert & Kim (Brookfield Place) 181 Bay St, Toronto, ON M5J 2T3
- **Cost:** Bowls and meals range from **$11-14 CAD**
- **How to get there:** Located in the heart of downtown, a short walk from

DINING ON A BUDGET

Union Station.

4. Veggie D'Light

If you're looking for cheap and filling vegan Caribbean food, head to **Veggie D'Light** in Kensington Market (160 Baldwin St, Toronto, ON M5T 3K7). This cozy spot offers flavorful dishes packed with spices and Caribbean flair, all at an affordable price.

- **Must-try dishes:** Their **Jamaican Patties** are a steal at **$5 CAD** and come stuffed with curried lentils, sweet potato, or chickpeas. The **Rasta Bowl**, which comes with rice and peas, sautéed vegetables, and a choice of protein like tofu or tempeh, costs about **$12 CAD**.
- **Why it's budget-friendly:** Veggie D'Light offers generous portions of delicious Caribbean-inspired vegan food at wallet-friendly prices. The meals are filling and healthy, making it one of the best-value options in the area.
- **Location:** Veggie D'Light, 160 Baldwin St, Toronto, ON M5T 3K7
- **Cost:** Dishes range from **$5-13 CAD**
- **How to get there:** It's located in Kensington Market, a short walk from the College St or Dundas St streetcar stops.

5. The Goods

For health-conscious travelers on a budget, **The Goods** (279 Roncesvalles Ave, Toronto, ON M6R 2M3) focuses on organic, plant-based meals made from scratch. They're known for their smoothies, soups, and bowls, which are both delicious and affordable.

- **Must-try dishes:** Their **Harvest Bowl**, with quinoa, kale, roasted sweet potatoes, and a tahini dressing, costs around **$14 CAD** and is perfect for a healthy, filling meal. Their **Super Green Smoothie** is another favorite, priced at **$8 CAD**, packed with spinach, kale, and avocado.

- **Why it's budget-friendly:** The Goods offers affordable, healthy meals that keep you full for hours. Their portions are generous, and the prices are reasonable given the quality of ingredients.
- **Location:** The Goods, 279 Roncesvalles Ave, Toronto, ON M6R 2M3
- **Cost:** Bowls and smoothies range from **$8-15 CAD**
- **How to get there:** Located in Roncesvalles Village, easily reachable by the Dundas West or 504 streetcars.

6. Urban Herbivore

Another Kensington Market favorite, **Urban Herbivore** (64 Oxford St, Toronto, ON M5T 1P3), is known for its fresh, made-to-order vegan salads, sandwiches, and bowls. If you're on a budget but still want a healthy, satisfying meal, this is a great spot to stop by.

- **Must-try dishes:** The **Build-Your-Own-Bowl** is a crowd favorite, allowing you to choose a base (like quinoa or rice), a protein (like tofu or tempeh), and a variety of vegetables and toppings, all for around **$13-15 CAD**. Their **Grain Bowls**, loaded with fresh ingredients, start at **$12 CAD**.
- **Why it's budget-friendly:** The build-your-own approach lets you control how much you spend based on what ingredients you choose. Plus, the portion sizes are generous, so you get a lot of value for the price.
- **Location:** Urban Herbivore, 64 Oxford St, Toronto, ON M5T 1P3
- **Cost:** Bowls range from **$12-15 CAD**
- **How to get there:** It's located in the heart of Kensington Market, a short walk from the Spadina streetcar.

7. Bunner's Bakeshop

For vegan travelers with a sweet tooth, **Bunner's Bakeshop** (244 Augusta Ave, Toronto, ON M5T 2L7) in Kensington Market is a must-visit. This

100% vegan and gluten-free bakery offers a range of affordable baked goods, perfect for a quick snack or dessert.

- **Must-try dishes:** Their famous **Cinnamon Buns** are just **$4.50 CAD** and are a perfect treat while walking around the market. If you're in the mood for something savory, their **Cheddar Herb Muffins** are priced at **$3.50 CAD** and make for a filling snack.
- **Why it's budget-friendly:** Bunner's keeps its prices affordable, making it easy to grab a snack or dessert without spending much. Plus, their baked goods are rich and satisfying, so even a small purchase goes a long way.
- **Location:** Bunner's Bakeshop, 244 Augusta Ave, Toronto, ON M5T 2L7
- **Cost:** Baked goods range from **$3-5 CAD**
- **How to get there:** Located in Kensington Market, easily accessible by the College or Dundas streetcar.

Budget-Friendly Attractions

Free Attractions and Sights in Toronto

1. **The Distillery District**

The **Distillery District** (55 Mill St, Toronto, ON M5A 3C4) is a pedestrian-only area filled with beautiful 19th-century architecture, art galleries, and small shops. It's completely free to walk around and explore. The district is known for its cobblestone streets and unique art installations, which change seasonally, so there's always something new to see.

- **What to do for free:** Walk through the district and admire the industrial-era architecture. Keep an eye out for public art displays, which are always interesting and great for photos. During the holiday season, the area turns into a winter wonderland with lights and free events, including a Christmas market.
- **How to get there:** It's easily reachable by streetcar. Take the **504 King Streetcar** to **Parliament Street** and walk a few minutes east.

2. **High Park**

One of Toronto's largest public parks, **High Park** (1873 Bloor St W, Toronto, ON M6R 2Z3) is a must-see for nature lovers. The park offers beautiful gardens, scenic walking trails, and even a small zoo—all free to enjoy. It's the perfect place to relax, have a picnic, or go for a hike.

BUDGET-FRIENDLY ATTRACTIONS

- **What to do for free:** Stroll through the **High Park Zoo**, which features animals like bison, capybaras, and peacocks. The zoo is free to enter year-round. In spring, the park is famous for its **cherry blossom trees**, drawing visitors from all over the city to see the beautiful blooms.
- **How to get there:** Take the **Line 2 subway** to **High Park Station**, and the park entrance is just a short walk away.

3. **Toronto Islands**

A ferry ride to the **Toronto Islands** (13-minute ride, $8.70 CAD round-trip) isn't free, but once you get there, exploring the islands doesn't cost a thing. The islands offer beaches, trails, and some of the best views of the Toronto skyline, making it well worth the small ferry fare.

- **What to do for free:** Walk or bike around the islands and enjoy the natural beauty. Visit the **Centre Island Beach** for a swim or relax at **Ward's Island** for a quieter, more peaceful setting. There are also picnic areas and plenty of open space for outdoor activities.
- **How to get there:** The ferry departs from the **Jack Layton Ferry Terminal** (9 Queens Quay W, Toronto, ON M5J 2H3). You can reach the terminal by walking from **Union Station** or taking the **Harbourfront streetcar**.

4. **St. Lawrence Market**

While you'll be tempted to buy something, it's free to walk around and take in the sights and smells at **St. Lawrence Market** (93 Front St E, Toronto, ON M5E 1C3). This historic market is one of the top food markets in the world and is filled with vendors selling fresh produce, artisanal goods, and local specialties.

- **What to do for free:** Wander through the aisles and sample the free food tastings often offered by vendors. The market is also a great place

to learn about the local culture and see how people in Toronto shop for fresh, local ingredients.
- **How to get there:** It's located a short walk from **Union Station** or the **King Street subway station**.

5. Nathan Phillips Square and Toronto Sign

If you're near **City Hall**, you'll find **Nathan Phillips Square** (100 Queen St W, Toronto, ON M5H 2N2), home to the famous **Toronto Sign**. This public square is a hub of activity, and there's always something happening here, whether it's free concerts, outdoor events, or just people watching.

- **What to do for free:** Take a photo with the **Toronto Sign**, explore the fountains, and enjoy the free performances often held in the square. In winter, there's free ice skating if you bring your own skates (skate rentals cost extra).
- **How to get there:** The square is located right in front of **City Hall**, at the corner of **Queen Street West** and **Bay Street**. It's easily accessible by subway from **Osgoode Station**.

6. Graffiti Alley

For street art lovers, **Graffiti Alley** (runs parallel to Queen St W, between Spadina Ave and Portland St) is a must-see. It's a colorful and vibrant stretch of alleyway where local artists create stunning murals. Walking through Graffiti Alley is a visual treat, and it's completely free.

- **What to do for free:** Walk through the alley and admire the constantly changing murals. You'll find everything from abstract designs to pop-culture-inspired art.
- **How to get there:** Graffiti Alley is located just off **Queen Street West**, and it's an easy walk from the **Spadina streetcar stop**.

BUDGET-FRIENDLY ATTRACTIONS

7. Trinity Bellwoods Park

For a relaxing afternoon, head to **Trinity Bellwoods Park** (790 Queen St W, Toronto, ON M6J 1G3), a favorite hangout spot for locals. It's perfect for picnics, people-watching, or just lounging in the sun. There are often free community events and performances happening in the park, especially in the summer.

- **What to do for free:** Bring a picnic and enjoy the open green space. You can also join in on the free activities like yoga sessions or community meetups that are held regularly.
- **How to get there:** Located along **Queen Street West**, the park is easily accessible by the **501 Queen streetcar**.

Museums and Galleries with Free or Discounted Entry

1. Art Gallery of Ontario (AGO)

The **Art Gallery of Ontario** (317 Dundas St W, Toronto, ON M5T 1G4) is one of the largest art museums in North America, and it's a must-visit for art lovers. The collection includes everything from Canadian art to contemporary pieces and European masterpieces.

- **Free entry opportunities:** Every Wednesday from **6:00 PM to 9:00 PM**, admission is free. This is the perfect time to explore the museum without spending any money. Make sure to arrive early, as the free admission evenings can get busy.
- **How to get there:** The AGO is located on **Dundas Street West**, near **St. Patrick subway station**.
- **Cost during other times:** General admission is **$25 CAD** for adults, but always check their website for special discounts or exhibitions.

Contact:

- Phone: +1 416-979-6648
- Website: AGO

2. Royal Ontario Museum (ROM)

The **Royal Ontario Museum** (100 Queens Park, Toronto, ON M5S 2C6) is famous for its vast collection of art, culture, and natural history. It's one of the top museums in Canada, offering something for every type of traveler, from dinosaur skeletons to ancient Egyptian artifacts.

- **Discounted entry opportunities:** The ROM offers **discounted admission on the third Monday of every month** from **5:30 PM to 8:30 PM**. During this time, you can explore the museum's permanent galleries at a reduced cost.
- **How to get there:** The ROM is located near **Museum Station** on the **Line 1 subway**.
- **Cost during other times:** Regular admission is **$23 CAD** for adults, but they often have special exhibitions that may be priced differently.

Contact:

- Phone: +1 416-586-8000
- Website: ROM

3. The Power Plant Contemporary Art Gallery

For those interested in contemporary art, the **Power Plant Contemporary Art Gallery** (231 Queens Quay W, Toronto, ON M5J 2G8) at the Harbourfront is a great stop. The gallery features works from both local and international artists and is dedicated to cutting-edge contemporary art.

- **Free entry opportunities:** Admission is always free, making it a perfect stop for budget travelers. In addition, they offer free guided tours on

BUDGET-FRIENDLY ATTRACTIONS

weekends at **2:00 PM** and **3:00 PM**, giving you more insight into the exhibitions.
- **How to get there:** Located on **Queens Quay West**, you can reach it via the **Harbourfront streetcar**.

Contact:

- Phone: +1 416-973-4949
- Website: The Power Plant

4. Bata Shoe Museum

The **Bata Shoe Museum** (327 Bloor St W, Toronto, ON M5S 1W7) is a quirky and unique museum dedicated to footwear from around the world. It's not free all the time, but they offer **"Pay-What-You-Can" Thursdays** from **5:00 PM to 8:00 PM**. You can visit the museum and pay whatever you're comfortable with, which can be a great deal for budget travelers.

- **How to get there:** The museum is located near **St. George Station** on the **Line 2 subway**.
- **Cost during other times:** General admission is **$14 CAD** for adults, but the Thursday evenings are your best bet for visiting on a budget.

Contact:

- Phone: +1 416-979-7799
- Website: Bata Shoe Museum

5. Textile Museum of Canada

The **Textile Museum of Canada** (55 Centre Ave, Toronto, ON M5G 2H5) is another lesser-known but fascinating spot to visit, showcasing textiles and fabrics from around the world. They offer **"Pay-What-You-Can"**

Wednesdays from **5:00 PM to 8:00 PM**.

- **How to get there:** The museum is located near **St. Patrick Station** on the **Line 1 subway**.
- **Cost during other times:** Regular admission is **$15 CAD** for adults, but the Wednesday evenings are an affordable way to check it out.

Contact:

- Phone: +1 416-599-5321
- Website: Textile Museum

Exploring Toronto's Parks: High Park, Toronto Islands, and More

1. High Park

High Park is the largest public park in Toronto and a favorite for both locals and visitors. It's located just west of downtown, and it's completely free to enter, making it one of the top budget-friendly destinations in the city. There's so much to see and do here that you can easily spend an entire day without spending a dime.

Sights not to miss:

- One of the highlights of High Park is the **High Park Zoo**. Yes, it's free! You can see animals like bison, llamas, peacocks, and even reindeer here. The zoo is small but charming, and it's a perfect stop if you're visiting with kids.
- Another must-see is the **Grenadier Pond**. It's a peaceful spot for walking, birdwatching, or just relaxing by the water. If you're visiting in the winter, the pond is open for ice skating, which is also free of charge.
- In the spring, the park is known for its **cherry blossoms**, which attract

a lot of visitors. The best time to see the cherry blossoms is usually in late April to early May. The trees are scattered throughout the park, but the main grove is near the **Grenadier Restaurant**.

Free activities:

- Aside from walking the scenic trails, High Park offers free tennis courts, picnic areas, and playgrounds. It's also home to **Shakespeare in the Park**, a free outdoor theatre performance that takes place in the summer months.

How to get there:

- High Park is easily accessible by public transit. You can take the **Line 2 (Bloor-Danforth)** subway to **High Park Station** or **Keele Station**, and the park is just a short walk from there.

Address:

- 1873 Bloor St W, Toronto, ON M6R 2Z3
- **Contact:** +1 416-338-0338
- **Cost:** Free

2. Toronto Islands

Just a short ferry ride away from downtown Toronto, the **Toronto Islands** are a perfect escape from the hustle and bustle of the city. While you do have to pay for the ferry ride (which costs **$8.70 CAD** for a round-trip), once you're on the islands, everything is free to enjoy. It's one of the best budget-friendly spots for a day out.

Sights not to miss:

- The islands offer stunning views of the Toronto skyline, and there are plenty of spots to take photos. **Centre Island Beach** is a must-visit, especially in the summer when you can swim, sunbathe, or simply relax by the water.
- If you're looking for a scenic walk, head to **Ward's Island**. This area is quieter than Centre Island, and it's great for a peaceful stroll. You'll pass by small cottages and beautiful gardens, and there are lots of benches to sit and enjoy the view.

Hanlan's Point is another area to explore. It's home to a clothing-optional beach, but even if that's not your thing, the surrounding park area is beautiful for walking or biking.

Free activities:

- The islands are perfect for hiking, biking, or picnicking. There are also free BBQ areas and playgrounds for families. If you visit during the summer, there are often free festivals and events happening on the islands.

How to get there:

- To reach the islands, you'll need to take the ferry from **Jack Layton Ferry Terminal**, located at the foot of Bay Street at Queen's Quay. The ferry ride takes about 15 minutes.

Address:

- Toronto Islands
- Ferry Terminal: 9 Queens Quay W, Toronto, ON M5J 2H3
- **Cost:** Ferry ride **$8.70 CAD** round trip for adults, free for kids under 14. Once on the islands, all activities are free.
- **Contact:** +1 416-392-8193

3. Trinity Bellwoods Park

Trinity Bellwoods Park is a hip, laid-back park located in the Queen West neighborhood. It's one of the most popular parks in the city, especially with young people and families. The park is known for its relaxed atmosphere, and it's completely free to enjoy.

Sights not to miss:

- One of the coolest things about Trinity Bellwoods is the "**White Squirrel**", a rare albino squirrel that has become a bit of a legend in the park. Keep an eye out while you're there! Another feature of the park is the **Garrison Creek**, a buried creek that's marked by a pathway running through the park. There's also a **community greenhouse**, which is great to check out if you're interested in urban gardening.

Free activities:

- The park has plenty of open space for picnics, frisbee, or just lounging in the sun. In the summer, there are often free yoga classes, concerts, and outdoor movie nights. The park also has free tennis courts, baseball diamonds, and even a skateboarding area.

How to get there:

- Take the **501 Queen** streetcar and get off at **Strachan Avenue**. The park is just a short walk from there.
- **Address:** 790 Queen St W, Toronto, ON M6J 1G3
- **Cost:** Free
- **Contact:** +1 416-392-1111

4. Riverdale Park East

If you're looking for one of the best views of the Toronto skyline,

Riverdale Park East is where you'll want to go. Located just east of the Don River, this park offers panoramic views of the city that are perfect for photo ops, especially at sunset. The park is a bit off the beaten path, so it's a quieter option for those looking to escape the crowds.

Sights not to miss:

- Aside from the stunning skyline views, Riverdale Park East is a great spot for picnics and walking. The park is also home to a working farm called **Riverdale Farm**, which is free to visit. You can see farm animals like goats, sheep, and chickens, making it a great spot for families.

Free activities:

- The park has a large open space for sports like soccer or frisbee, as well as a walking path that takes you through the green hills. In the winter, the park becomes one of the best spots for tobogganing in the city.

How to get there:

- Take the **504 King** streetcar east to **Broadview Avenue** and walk up the hill to the park.

Address:

- 550 Broadview Ave, Toronto, ON M4K 2N6
- **Cost:** Free
- **Contact:** +1 416-392-6794

BUDGET-FRIENDLY ATTRACTIONS

Free Walking Tours and Scenic Routes

1. The ROMwalks (Royal Ontario Museum)

The **ROMwalks** are free walking tours offered by the Royal Ontario Museum. These guided tours take you through different neighborhoods and areas of historical interest, and the guides are knowledgeable volunteers from the museum.

What you'll see:

- There are different themes depending on the tour you choose. For example, the **Yorkville** tour explores the old bohemian area of Toronto, where artists and musicians like Neil Young used to hang out. Another popular tour is **The Annex**, a historical neighborhood filled with grand homes and interesting architecture.

Why it's budget-friendly:

- The tours are completely free, though donations to the ROM are appreciated. It's a great way to learn about Toronto's history while enjoying a walk through different parts of the city.

How to join:

- Check the **ROMwalks schedule** on the Royal Ontario Museum's website. Tours usually run from May to October and last about 90 minutes.
- **Website:** ROMwalks
- **Cost:** Free, though donations are appreciated.

2. The PATH: Toronto's Underground City

Toronto's **PATH** is the largest underground shopping complex in the world, but it's also a great route for exploring downtown Toronto, especially if you want to avoid cold or rainy weather. The PATH is completely free to walk through, and it connects many of Toronto's major landmarks.

What you'll see:

- As you walk through the PATH, you'll pass through downtown office buildings, shopping centers, and food courts. Some key landmarks you can connect to include **Union Station, Eaton Centre, City Hall**, and **Nathan Phillips Square**. While most people think of the PATH as a way to shop, it's also a great route for seeing the city from a different perspective.

Why it's budget-friendly:

- Walking through the PATH is free, and there are plenty of places to stop and rest. It's a perfect route during the colder months when outdoor walking tours aren't as enjoyable.

How to navigate:

- You can enter the PATH from multiple locations downtown, including **Union Station** and **Eaton Centre**. There are maps posted throughout the underground system to help guide you.
- **Cost:** Free

3. **Kensington Market Self-Guided Tour**

If you prefer to explore on your own, a **self-guided tour of Kensington Market** is a great option. Kensington Market is one of Toronto's most unique and diverse neighborhoods, known for its eclectic shops, vibrant street art, and international food stalls. You can easily spend a few hours wandering through the market on foot, taking in the sights and sounds.

What you'll see:

- Start your walk at **Spadina Avenue** and **Dundas Street West** and make your way into the heart of the market. Be sure to check out **Augusta Avenue**, where you'll find plenty of colorful murals and street art. You'll also pass by vintage clothing shops, cafes, and small grocery stores selling international foods.

Why it's budget-friendly:

- The entire area is walkable, and you don't need to spend any money to enjoy the atmosphere. Even if you don't buy anything, Kensington Market is full of sights and people-watching opportunities.

How to get there:

- Take the **Spadina streetcar** and get off at **Dundas Street West**. From there, it's just a short walk to the market.
- **Cost:** Free

Budget Tips for Iconic Landmarks

1. CN Tower

The **CN Tower** (301 Front St W, Toronto, ON M5V 2T6) is one of Toronto's most famous landmarks, and it offers stunning views of the city and Lake Ontario. However, the entry fee can be a bit steep for budget travelers. Thankfully, there are ways to get the CN Tower experience without paying full price.

- **Regular ticket prices:** The standard entry fee to the CN Tower's **LookOut Level** is **$43 CAD** for adults. If you want to go to the **SkyPod**, it's an additional **$15 CAD**. While the views are fantastic, paying over $50 for a visit can be tough if you're on a budget.

Budget Tip 1: Go during off-peak hours

- If you're flexible, visiting the CN Tower early in the morning or later in the evening can sometimes score you a less crowded experience. While this doesn't necessarily lower the ticket price, it allows you to make the most of your visit without the long lines.

Budget Tip 2: Combine tickets

- The CN Tower offers combination tickets that include other attractions like **Ripley's Aquarium of Canada** (288 Bremner Blvd, Toronto, ON M5V 3L9), which is located right next door. By bundling your visit, you can save around **10-15%** on tickets. It's a great way to stretch your budget if you were planning on visiting both attractions anyway. The **CityPass** is another option that bundles five attractions, including the CN Tower, for **$104 CAD** for adults, which saves you up to **40%** compared to individual tickets.

Budget Tip 3: Special offers and discounts

- Keep an eye out for deals on platforms like **Groupon**, where you can sometimes find discounted tickets for the CN Tower. Also, if you have an **ISIC student card** or are a member of **CAA** (Canadian Automobile Association), you may be eligible for discounts.

How to get there: The CN Tower is centrally located in downtown Toronto, a short walk from **Union Station**. You can take the TTC subway to Union Station and then walk west along Front Street.

2. Distillery District

The **Distillery District** (55 Mill St, Toronto, ON M5A 3C4) is a historic area known for its cobblestone streets, art galleries, and beautifully preserved Victorian industrial architecture. The best part? Walking around the Distillery District is completely free. It's a perfect place to explore on foot, with no need to spend money unless you choose to shop or dine.

Budget Tip 1: Explore for free

- You don't need to spend a dime to enjoy the Distillery District. Simply walking through the area, admiring the art installations, and taking in the historic atmosphere is an experience in itself. The district is particularly beautiful during the holidays when it's decorated with lights and hosts the **Toronto Christmas Market**, which is free to enter on weekdays.

Budget Tip 2: Visit during free events

- The Distillery District often hosts free public events, especially during the summer. Keep an eye out for art festivals, live music performances, and outdoor markets. Many of these events don't require any ticket or admission fee, so you can enjoy the vibe without spending much.
- **How to get there:** The Distillery District is located east of downtown Toronto. You can take the **504 King streetcar** and get off at the **Distillery Loop**, which drops you right at the entrance to the district.

3. Royal Ontario Museum (ROM)

The **Royal Ontario Museum (ROM)** (100 Queens Park, Toronto, ON M5S 2C6) is one of Canada's largest and most renowned museums, featuring everything from dinosaurs to ancient Egyptian artifacts. While regular admission can add up, there are ways to explore the ROM on a budget.

- **Regular ticket prices:** General admission to the ROM is **$23 CAD** for adults. Special exhibits often come with an extra fee, which can make a visit more expensive.

Budget Tip 1: Visit on the third Monday of the month

- The ROM offers **free admission** to the museum's permanent galleries on the third Monday of each month from **5:30 PM to 8:30 PM**. This is a fantastic way to explore the museum's collections without paying the regular entry fee.

Budget Tip 2: Get discounted tickets with CityPass

- The ROM is part of the **CityPass** Toronto bundle, so if you're planning on visiting multiple attractions like the CN Tower and the **Toronto Zoo**, this can save you money overall. The **CityPass** costs **$104 CAD** and covers five major attractions.

How to get there: The ROM is located in the **University of Toronto** district, and it's easily accessible by TTC. Take the **Line 1 subway** to **Museum Station**, which is just steps from the museum entrance.

4. **Toronto Islands**

The **Toronto Islands** are one of the city's best outdoor attractions and a fantastic budget-friendly destination. The islands are just a short ferry ride from the city, but they feel a world away, offering beaches, picnic spots, and biking trails.

Cost: A round-trip ferry ticket to the Toronto Islands costs **$8.70 CAD** for adults, **$5.60 CAD** for seniors, and **$4.10 CAD** for children under 14. Once you're on the islands, most activities are free, including access to the beaches, parks, and walking trails.

Budget Tip 1: Bring your own picnic

- Food and drink prices on the islands can be a little higher than in the city, so pack your own picnic and enjoy it at one of the many picnic tables or grassy areas. It's a great way to save money while enjoying the beautiful scenery.

Budget Tip 2: Rent a bike

- If you want to explore the islands at a faster pace, renting a bike is an affordable and eco-friendly option. Bike rentals cost around **$9 CAD per hour** or **$36 CAD for the day.** You can rent bikes at **Toronto Island Bicycle Rental** near **Centre Island**.

How to get there: Ferries to the Toronto Islands depart from the **Jack Layton Ferry Terminal** (9 Queens Quay W, Toronto, ON M5J 2H3). You can reach the ferry terminal by walking from **Union Station** or taking the **Harbourfront streetcar.**

5. Art Gallery of Ontario (AGO)

The **Art Gallery of Ontario (AGO)** (317 Dundas St W, Toronto, ON M5T 1G4) is one of the largest art museums in North America, with a collection that spans centuries of art history. Although regular admission is priced at **$25 CAD** for adults, there are several ways to visit the AGO without spending much.

Budget Tip 1: Free Wednesdays

- The AGO offers **free admission** to its permanent collections every Wednesday from **6:00 PM to 9:00 PM**. This is a fantastic opportunity to explore the museum's vast collection of Canadian and international art without paying the full entry fee.

Budget Tip 2: AGO Annual Pass

- If you're staying in Toronto for a longer period or plan to visit multiple times, the **AGO Annual Pass** is a budget-friendly option. For just **$35 CAD** a year, you get unlimited admission to the museum and access to special exhibitions.

How to get there: The AGO is located in downtown Toronto, near **Chinatown** and **Kensington Market**. Take the **501 Queen streetcar** or the **505 Dundas streetcar** to get there.

6. **Casa Loma**

Casa Loma (1 Austin Terrace, Toronto, ON M5R 1X8) is a Gothic Revival-style mansion that offers visitors a glimpse into Toronto's past. Although it's one of the city's more expensive attractions, there are ways to visit without overspending.

Regular ticket prices: General admission to Casa Loma is **$30 CAD** for adults. While this is on the pricier side for a budget traveler, it's worth it if you're interested in history and architecture.

Budget Tip 1: Check for discounts

- Casa Loma sometimes offers **seasonal promotions** or discounts through platforms like **Groupon**, so it's worth checking these sites before you book. Additionally, the **CityPass** includes Casa Loma as one of its five attractions, so you can save money if you're visiting other sites too.

Budget Tip 2: Visit the gardens

- If you don't want to pay for full admission, consider visiting the Casa Loma gardens, which are free to explore in the summer months. The gardens are beautifully maintained, and you'll still get a glimpse of the mansion's stunning exterior.

How to get there: Casa Loma is located in midtown Toronto, near **Dupont Station** on the **Line 1 subway**. From the station, it's about a 10-minute walk uphill to the mansion.

7. St. Lawrence Market

St. Lawrence Market (93 Front St E, Toronto, ON M5E 1C3) is one of the best places in Toronto to experience local food and culture without spending a lot. It's free to enter, and you can easily spend a few hours wandering through the market, tasting samples, and enjoying the atmosphere.

Budget Tip 1: Sample before you buy

- Many vendors at St. Lawrence Market offer free samples of their products, from cheeses to pastries. This is a great way to try a variety of local foods without spending money. When you do decide to buy, stick to smaller, budget-friendly snacks like **peameal bacon sandwiches**, which go for around **$6-7 CAD**.

Budget Tip 2: Visit on weekdays

- The market can get crowded on weekends, but visiting during the week often means shorter lines and the chance to chat with vendors. Sometimes, towards the end of the day, vendors offer discounts on perishables to avoid waste.
- **How to get there:** St. Lawrence Market is located in downtown Toronto, easily accessible by the **King streetcar** or a short walk from **Union Station**.

Shopping on a Budget

Budget Shopping Districts: Kensington Market, Queen Street West

1. **Kensington Market**

Kensington Market (Spadina Ave & Dundas St W, Toronto, ON M5T 2E9) is one of the most eclectic and vibrant neighborhoods in Toronto. Known for its bohemian atmosphere, Kensington is a great place to shop if you're looking for budget-friendly items, whether it's vintage clothes, handmade jewelry, or affordable international food.

What to expect: The streets are lined with quirky independent shops, cafes, and street vendors selling everything from secondhand books to handmade crafts. The vibe here is laid-back and unpretentious, making it the perfect spot for travelers who want to wander, explore, and find deals.

Budget-friendly stores:

- **Exile Vintage** (20 Kensington Ave) – A well-known shop for vintage lovers, Exile carries a wide range of clothing and accessories from the '60s to '90s. Prices for jackets, dresses, and boots are usually around **$20-50 CAD**, but if you visit during their sales, you can score items for much less.
- **Courage My Love** (14 Kensington Ave) – Another vintage gem in Kensington Market, this shop is known for its unique selection of

accessories, beads, and trinkets. Whether you're looking for jewelry or small decor items, prices here are reasonable, with many pieces under **$10 CAD**.

- **Bungalow** (273 Augusta Ave) – A blend of modern and vintage, Bungalow offers clothing, furniture, and home decor items at affordable prices. You can find vintage jeans for around **$30 CAD**, and retro furniture at a fraction of the cost compared to big stores.
- **Food markets:** While you're in Kensington, don't forget to check out the food markets for budget-friendly snacks and groceries. **Sanagan's Meat Locker** (176 Baldwin St) is a popular spot for locals, and you can grab delicious meats and cheeses at a good price.
- **Why shop here:** Kensington Market is a treasure trove for budget travelers. You'll find unique items you won't see in big chain stores, and the prices are often negotiable. It's also a great area to visit if you love supporting small businesses and independent sellers.
- **How to get there:** Take the **510 Spadina streetcar** and get off at **Spadina and Dundas**. From there, it's a short walk to Kensington Market, where you can easily explore on foot.

2. Queen Street West

Queen Street West (Queen St W between Spadina Ave and Dufferin St) is another shopping haven in Toronto that's perfect for budget-conscious travelers. It's known for its trendy boutiques, independent stores, and vibrant street art. While some parts of Queen West cater to higher-end fashion, there are plenty of affordable stores where you can find stylish clothing, shoes, and accessories without spending a fortune.

What to expect: This area is trendy and artsy, with a mix of indie boutiques, vintage shops, and street vendors. The vibe is young and energetic, and it's the kind of place where you can find a mix of high-end and budget-friendly options.

Budget-friendly stores:

- **Black Market Clothing** (256 Queen St W) – One of the best-known budget stores in Queen West, Black Market is famous for its **$10 CAD** racks. The store is massive, and you can find everything from graphic tees to leather jackets at incredibly low prices.
- **Public Butter** (1290 Queen St W) – A little further west, Public Butter is a great spot for vintage clothing and housewares. It's well-organized and affordable, with items like flannels, denim, and bomber jackets ranging from **$15-40 CAD**.
- **Rock 'N' Karma** (789 Queen St W) – If you're looking for something a little more unique but still within budget, Rock 'N' Karma offers bold, artistic fashion pieces at reasonable prices. Their clearance rack often features markdowns that can bring prices down to around **$30-50 CAD**.
- **Why shop here:** Queen Street West is a great place for travelers who want to blend trendy shopping with budget finds. You can pick up stylish items that look expensive but are actually quite affordable. Plus, the street itself is full of art, cafes, and live performances, making it a fun shopping destination.
- **How to get there:** Take the **501 Queen streetcar** and hop off anywhere between **Spadina Ave** and **Dufferin St** to explore the wide range of shops.

Vintage Shops and Thrift Stores for Unique Bargains

If you're a fan of vintage clothing and thrift stores, Toronto has some of the best spots to find unique items at affordable prices. Whether you're after retro fashion, classic vinyl records, or quirky home decor, there's something for every thrifty traveler.

1. **Exile Vintage**

Located in the heart of Kensington Market, **Exile Vintage** (20 Kensin Ave) is a top destination for vintage lovers. The shop is packed with clothi. from the '60s, '70s, '80s, and '90s, offering everything from denim jackets to retro dresses.

- **What to find:** Exile is known for its extensive selection of leather jackets, vintage boots, and one-of-a-kind accessories. Prices are reasonable for vintage, with leather jackets going for around **$50-100 CAD**, and vintage band tees starting at **$20 CAD**.
- **Why it's budget-friendly:** Vintage clothing can be pricey in some cities, but Exile offers a wide range of items that are affordable, especially if you're willing to hunt through the racks for hidden gems. They often have sales where you can find even bigger bargains.

2. Public Butter

Public Butter (1290 Queen St W, Toronto, ON M6K 1L4) is a vintage store located on the west end of Queen Street West, and it's a must-visit if you're into retro clothing and collectibles. The store is spacious and organized, making it easy to browse through their large inventory.

- **What to find:** Public Butter is well-known for its selection of vintage Levi's denim, flannels, and leather jackets. Prices are affordable, with jeans typically priced around **$30-40 CAD** and vintage tees starting at **$15 CAD**.
- **Why it's budget-friendly:** The store frequently runs sales where you can score even better deals on already affordable items. It's also a great place for those looking for unique home decor items or vintage vinyl records.
- **How to get there:** Public Butter is located in Parkdale, a bit further west on Queen Street. You can take the **501 Queen streetcar** and get off at **Brock Avenue**.

...gton Market is **Courage My Love** (14 Kensington ... 2L6). This quirky store has been around for decades with vintage jewelry, beads, clothing, and accessories.

- **What to find:** Courage My Love is especially popular for its selection of vintage jewelry and unique trinkets. You'll find plenty of affordable items, like rings and necklaces priced between **$5-20 CAD**, as well as vintage clothing starting at **$15 CAD**.
- **Why it's budget-friendly:** Unlike some vintage stores that charge high prices for unique pieces, Courage My Love keeps its items reasonably priced, making it a favorite for budget-conscious shoppers looking for something truly special.

4. The Salvation Army Thrift Store

For travelers who enjoy thrifting, the **Salvation Army Thrift Store** (1447 Queen St W, Toronto, ON M6K 1M5) is a solid choice for budget shopping. The store is well-organized and offers everything from clothing to furniture at bargain prices.

- **What to find:** You'll find secondhand clothing, shoes, and accessories, with prices starting as low as **$5 CAD** for tops and **$10 CAD** for dresses. The store also has a section for home goods and furniture, where you can pick up affordable decor items.
- **Why it's budget-friendly:** Thrift stores like Salvation Army are ideal for travelers who want to save money while shopping for basic wardrobe staples or unique finds. The prices are unbeatable, and you never know what hidden gems you might find.
- **How to get there:** The Salvation Army Thrift Store is located on Queen Street West, just west of Dufferin. Take the **501 Queen streetcar** and get off at **Lansdowne Ave**.

SHOPPING ON A BUDGET

5. Black Market Clothing

If you're looking for serious bargains, **Black Market Clothing** (256 Queen St W, Toronto, ON M5V 1Z8) is the place to go. Everything in the store is priced at **$10 CAD**, making it one of the cheapest places to shop for vintage and thrift clothing in Toronto.

- **What to find:** Black Market has a massive selection of items, from graphic tees to military jackets, jeans, and flannel shirts. You can find unique items like band tees, quirky sweaters, and vintage dresses, all for just **$10 CAD**.
- **Why it's budget-friendly:** Black Market is one of the most affordable vintage stores in Toronto, and with everything priced at **$10 CAD**, it's easy to pick up multiple items without worrying about your budget. The store is particularly popular with students and budget travelers.
- **How to get there:** Black Market is located on Queen Street West, just a short walk from **Osgoode subway station**. You can also take the **501 Queen streetcar** and get off at **John Street**.

Where to Find Local Art, Crafts, and Souvenirs on a Budget

1. Kensington Market

Kensington Market (Spadina Ave & Dundas St W, Toronto, ON M5T 2E9) is one of the most eclectic and affordable places to shop for local art, crafts, and unique souvenirs. This vibrant neighborhood is full of independent vendors and small shops that sell everything from handmade jewelry to vintage clothes, making it a great place to find one-of-a-kind items at budget-friendly prices.

- **Budget Tip:** Take your time wandering through the market's winding streets. Some of the best deals can be found in smaller shops tucked away in alleyways or side streets. Look for handmade jewelry, custom

art prints, and quirky souvenirs priced around **$10-20 CAD.**
- **What to buy:** Local prints, handcrafted jewelry, and artisanal food items like honey or jams.
- **Why it's budget-friendly:** Most vendors are independent, and prices are often lower than what you'd find in tourist-heavy areas. Plus, many items are handmade, so you're getting a unique piece without paying high-end prices.
- **Location:** Kensington Market, Spadina Ave & Dundas St W
- **How to get there:** Take the **Spadina streetcar** to **Kensington Market** and explore the area on foot.

2. **The Distillery District's Artscape Shops**

While the **Distillery District** (55 Mill St, Toronto, ON M5A 3C4) is known for its historic charm and upscale galleries, it's also home to several budget-friendly arts and craft shops. The **Artscape Distillery Studios** house local artists and craftsmen who sell handmade items at reasonable prices.

- **Budget Tip:** If you're looking for unique pieces of art or handcrafted items, check out **Artscape Distillery Studios.** Many artists sell directly from their studios, so prices are often lower than in larger galleries. You can find small art prints for around **$20 CAD** or handmade ceramics starting at **$15 CAD.**
- **What to buy:** Handcrafted pottery, small sculptures, and locally made prints.
- **Why it's budget-friendly:** You're buying directly from the artist, which cuts out the middleman and makes it more affordable. Plus, browsing the Distillery District is free, so you can take your time exploring without any pressure to spend.
- **Location:** Distillery District, 55 Mill St, Toronto, ON M5A 3C4
- **How to get there:** Take the **504 King streetcar** to the **Distillery Loop** and walk from there.

3. St. Lawrence Market

St. Lawrence Market (93 Front St E, Toronto, ON M5E 1C3) is one of Toronto's best-known markets, and while it's famous for its food stalls, it's also a great spot to find affordable local crafts and souvenirs. Many of the vendors sell handmade items, from woodwork to textiles, and prices are reasonable compared to other markets.

- **Budget Tip:** Visit on a weekday to avoid crowds and spend time browsing the different craft stalls. Many vendors are willing to negotiate, especially if you're buying multiple items. You can find locally made wooden kitchenware, leather goods, or small art prints for **$10-30 CAD**.
- **What to buy:** Handmade wooden crafts, leather goods, and Canadian-themed souvenirs.
- **Why it's budget-friendly:** The market is full of local artisans who set their own prices, so you can often find good deals. Plus, there's no entry fee, so it's free to explore.
- **Location:** 93 Front St E, Toronto, ON M5E 1C3
- **How to get there:** Take the **King streetcar** to **Jarvis St** or walk from **Union Station**.

4. Toronto Art Crawl

If you're in Toronto at the right time, the **Toronto Art Crawl** is an excellent way to find local art and crafts at budget-friendly prices. This outdoor market showcases the work of local artists and artisans, offering everything from paintings to handmade jewelry.

- **Budget Tip:** Visit the Art Crawl towards the end of the day when vendors are more likely to offer discounts on items to avoid packing them up. You can find small art prints for **$15-20 CAD** and handmade jewelry starting at **$10 CAD**.
- **What to buy:** Paintings, jewelry, ceramics, and unique handmade gifts.
- **Why it's budget-friendly:** Many vendors at the Art Crawl are emerging

artists who price their work affordably to attract new buyers.
- **Location:** Various locations across Toronto
- **How to get there:** Check the event's website for specific locations and times. Public transit options vary depending on the event's venue.

Shopping Deals: Discount Outlets and Seasonal Markets

1. Toronto Premium Outlets

Located just outside of the city in **Halton Hills**, the **Toronto Premium Outlets** (13850 Steeles Ave W, Halton Hills, ON L7G 0J1) is one of the best places to find discounts on brand-name items. With over 80 stores offering up to 65% off regular retail prices, it's a great spot to find deals on clothing, accessories, and shoes.

- **Budget Tip:** The best time to shop at Toronto Premium Outlets is during **long weekends** and **holiday sales**, when stores offer additional discounts on already reduced prices. Check the outlet's website for sales events before you go. You can find deals on brand-name clothing starting at **$10-20 CAD**.
- **What to buy:** Clothing, accessories, shoes, and luggage at a fraction of the original price.
- **Why it's budget-friendly:** Outlet stores offer significant discounts on high-quality items, so it's possible to buy designer goods at lower prices than in the city.
- **Location:** 13850 Steeles Ave W, Halton Hills, ON L7G 0J1
- **How to get there:** From downtown Toronto, take the **Go Transit bus** from Union Station to **Toronto Premium Outlets**. The trip takes about 45 minutes.

2. Orfus Road Outlet District

SHOPPING ON A BUDGET

Closer to downtown, the **Orfus Road Outlet District** (Orfus Rd, Toronto, ON M6A 1L6) is a hidden gem for bargain hunters. This area is lined with outlet stores that offer steep discounts on clothing, shoes, and home goods. You'll find both local and international brands at a fraction of their original cost.

- **Budget Tip:** Shop on weekdays when the stores are less crowded, and you'll have more time to browse the racks. Many stores also offer additional markdowns at the end of the season, so it's worth visiting in the **late summer or early winter** for the best deals.
- **What to buy:** Discounted clothing, shoes, home goods, and accessories. You can find jeans for **$15-20 CAD** and shoes starting at **$20 CAD**.
- **Why it's budget-friendly:** The Orfus Road Outlet District is home to outlet versions of popular stores like **Winners** and **Urban Planet**, where you can find brand-name goods at heavily discounted prices.
- **Location:** Orfus Rd, Toronto, ON M6A 1L6
- **How to get there:** Take the **29 Dufferin bus** north to **Orfus Rd**, or take the **Line 1 subway** to **Yorkdale Station** and walk from there.

3. The Leslieville Flea

For a more unique shopping experience, head to **The Leslieville Flea**, a seasonal market that features vintage goods, handmade crafts, and affordable local art. The flea market pops up at different locations throughout the year, often in the **Distillery District** or along **Queen St East**.

- **Budget Tip:** Visit at the end of the day when vendors may be more willing to negotiate prices. You can find vintage clothing for **$10-20 CAD** and handmade crafts starting at **$5 CAD**.
- **What to buy:** Vintage clothes, handmade crafts, jewelry, and one-of-a-kind souvenirs.
- **Why it's budget-friendly:** Many of the items at the Leslieville Flea are second-hand or made by local artisans, meaning you can find unique

pieces at a lower cost than in regular stores.
- **Location:** Various locations throughout the year
- **How to get there:** Check the flea market's website for dates and locations, and take public transit depending on the venue.

4. Toronto Christmas Market (Distillery District)

If you're visiting Toronto during the holiday season, the **Toronto Christmas Market** in the **Distillery District** is a must-visit for budget-conscious shoppers. While it's free to enter on weekdays, you can browse stalls selling locally made crafts, food, and holiday gifts.

- **Budget Tip:** Visit during **weekday afternoons** for free entry and less crowded shopping. Many vendors offer small items like handmade ornaments or candles for **$5-10 CAD**, which make for great souvenirs or gifts.
- **What to buy:** Handmade holiday gifts, ornaments, and artisanal food items.
- **Why it's budget-friendly:** The market features a wide range of price points, so even if you're on a tight budget, you'll find something affordable to bring home.
- **Location:** Distillery District, 55 Mill St, Toronto, ON M5A 3C4
- **How to get there:** Take the **504 King streetcar** to the **Distillery Loop**.

Nightlife and Entertainment

Affordable Bars and Lounges in Toronto

1. The Green Room

The Green Room (414 College St, Toronto, ON M5T 1T3) is a hidden gem in the heart of **Kensington Market**. This artsy, laid-back bar offers affordable drinks in a cozy, vintage setting. It's a popular spot among students and young professionals, known for its cheap cocktails, dim lighting, and outdoor patio.

- **Budget Tip:** The Green Room is known for its **$6-8 CAD cocktails** and pints of beer, making it one of the best spots for a cheap night out. Happy hours run every day, so it's a great time to get even better deals on drinks.
- **What makes it ideal for budget travelers:** The atmosphere is relaxed, and the prices are hard to beat in a city where drinks can get expensive. It's a great place to hang out with friends or meet fellow travelers in an unpretentious setting.
- **Location:** 414 College St, Toronto, ON M5T 1T3
- **Cost:** Cocktails for **$6-8 CAD**, pints for **$7 CAD**
- **How to get there:** Take the **College streetcar** to Kensington Market and walk a couple of blocks to find this hidden spot.

2. Sneaky Dee's

If you're into live music and Tex-Mex food, **Sneaky Dee's** (431 College St, Toronto, ON M5T 1T1) is a Toronto institution. Located in **Little Italy**, it's a budget-friendly spot for those who want a loud and lively atmosphere with cheap drinks and live music. Sneaky Dee's often hosts punk rock shows, and its upstairs music venue is a great place to catch a live performance without breaking the bank.

- **Budget Tip:** They're known for their **$5.50 CAD bottles of beer** and **cheap tequila shots**. If you're hungry, their famous **King's Crown Nachos** are perfect for sharing and cost about **$15 CAD**, which can easily feed two or three people.
- **What makes it ideal for budget travelers:** Between the affordable drinks, filling food, and live music, Sneaky Dee's is the perfect place for budget-conscious travelers who want to experience Toronto's nightlife without overspending.
- **Location:** 431 College St, Toronto, ON M5T 1T1
- **Cost:** Bottles of beer for **$5.50 CAD**, nachos for **$15 CAD**
- **How to get there:** Take the **506 College streetcar** to College and Bathurst.

3. The Done Right Inn

If you're looking for an inexpensive, no-frills bar, **The Done Right Inn** (861 Queen St W, Toronto, ON M6J 1G4) is a great option. Located on **Queen Street West**, this dive bar offers cheap drinks and a laid-back atmosphere with a big outdoor patio.

- **Budget Tip:** The Done Right Inn has pints for around **$6 CAD**, and they don't charge cover on weekends. It's a great place to grab a cheap drink before heading out to explore other spots on Queen West.
- **What makes it ideal for budget travelers:** With affordable drinks and a welcoming vibe, this is a solid option for travelers who want a casual,

NIGHTLIFE AND ENTERTAINMENT

unpretentious spot to enjoy a night out in one of Toronto's trendiest neighborhoods.
- **Location:** 861 Queen St W, Toronto, ON M6J 1G4
- **Cost:** Pints for **$6 CAD**
- **How to get there:** Take the **501 Queen streetcar** to Queen St W and Bellwoods Ave.

4. Bar Hop

For craft beer lovers on a budget, **Bar Hop** (391 King St W, Toronto, ON M5V 1K1) is the place to go. With multiple locations around the city, Bar Hop offers a wide selection of local and international craft beers at reasonable prices. The atmosphere is lively but casual, making it perfect for budget travelers who want to try different brews without overspending.

- **Budget Tip:** Look for the **happy hour specials**, where pints of craft beer can go for as low as **$5 CAD**. They also have a **late-night menu** with discounted snacks, including fries and wings for **$6-8 CAD**.
- **What makes it ideal for budget travelers:** You get to try a variety of craft beers without paying the premium prices that are often associated with craft beer spots. The friendly, relaxed atmosphere also makes it easy to chat with other patrons and bartenders.
- **Location:** 391 King St W, Toronto, ON M5V 1K1
- **Cost:** Pints for **$5-8 CAD**
- **How to get there:** Take the **504 King streetcar** to King and Spadina.

5. The Cloak Bar

If you're looking for a bit of mystery without the high prices, check out **The Cloak Bar** (488 Wellington St W, Toronto, ON M5V 1E3), a speakeasy-style bar tucked away beneath **Marben Restaurant**. It offers a unique atmosphere, perfect for a cozy night out with reasonably priced drinks in a more upscale setting.

- **Budget Tip:** Cocktails here are priced around **$10-12 CAD**, which is a steal considering the quality and atmosphere. It's a great place to experience a speakeasy vibe without the hefty price tag.
- **What makes it ideal for budget travelers:** The Cloak Bar gives you the feel of a high-end cocktail lounge but at a much more affordable price. It's a hidden gem for travelers looking for a unique spot to enjoy well-crafted drinks without overspending.
- **Location:** 488 Wellington St W, Toronto, ON M5V 1E3
- **Cost:** Cocktails for **$10-12 CAD**
- **How to get there:** Take the **King streetcar** to Bathurst, then walk south on Wellington.

Free Outdoor Concerts and Festivals: Enjoy Toronto's Music Scene

1. Toronto Music Garden Summer Concert Series

The **Toronto Music Garden** (479 Queens Quay W, Toronto, ON M5V 2Y3) is a beautiful outdoor venue located along the waterfront, and every summer it hosts a series of free concerts. The concerts range from classical to world music, and the setting is stunning, with the lake as a backdrop.

- **Budget Tip:** Bring a blanket and a picnic, and enjoy the concert on the grass. It's a completely free event, and you can take in the performances while relaxing in the park.
- **Why it's perfect for budget travelers:** It's an ideal way to experience live music in a peaceful, scenic setting without spending any money. You can also take a walk along the waterfront before or after the concert for a perfect evening out.
- **Location:** 479 Queens Quay W, Toronto, ON M5V 2Y3
- **Cost:** Free
- **How to get there:** Take the **509 Harbourfront streetcar** to Queens Quay and Spadina, then walk west along the waterfront.

2. Beaches International Jazz Festival

Every July, the **Beaches International Jazz Festival** takes over **The Beaches** neighborhood, offering free live performances at several outdoor stages. The festival features a mix of jazz, blues, reggae, and more, making it one of Toronto's most popular free music events.

- **Budget Tip:** The festival is completely free to attend, and since it's held outdoors, you can wander between stages and check out different performances at your own pace. It's also a great place to discover up-and-coming artists.
- **Why it's perfect for budget travelers:** You get access to multiple days of live music without paying for tickets, and the festival atmosphere is electric. There's also no need to spend money on food and drinks if you pack your own snacks and picnic at **Woodbine Park** during the shows.
- **Location:** The Beaches, Toronto (main stage at Woodbine Park)
- **Cost:** Free
- **How to get there:** Take the **501 Queen streetcar** east to The Beaches and walk to **Woodbine Park**.

3. Harbourfront Centre Summer Music in the Garden

Every summer, **Harbourfront Centre** (235 Queens Quay W, Toronto, ON M5J 2G8) hosts **Summer Music in the Garden**, a free concert series that takes place in a beautiful outdoor setting right by the lake. The performances range from classical to folk music, with talented local and international musicians taking the stage.

- **Budget Tip:** The concerts are free, and you can bring your own food and drinks to enjoy during the performances. Arrive early to get a good spot, as these events can get busy, especially on weekends.
- **Why it's perfect for budget travelers:** It's one of the best ways to enjoy high-quality live music for free, all while soaking in the waterfront views. Plus, there are plenty of free events happening at Harbourfront Centre

year-round, so there's always something to check out.
- **Location:** 235 Queens Quay W, Toronto, ON M5J 2G8
- **Cost:** Free
- **How to get there:** Take the **509 Harbourfront streetcar** to Harbourfront Centre.

4. Indie Fridays at Yonge-Dundas Square

Yonge-Dundas Square (1 Dundas St E, Toronto, ON M5B 2R8) hosts **Indie Fridays** during the summer, a series of free outdoor concerts featuring independent and emerging artists. The concerts take place right in the heart of downtown, and the genres range from indie rock to hip-hop and everything in between.

- **Budget Tip:** Since the concerts are held in the middle of downtown, it's easy to combine this with other free activities, like exploring **Nathan Phillips Square** or walking around **Eaton Centre**. You can also grab affordable street food from nearby vendors to enjoy during the show.
- **Why it's perfect for budget travelers:** Indie Fridays are a great way to discover new music for free, all while being in the bustling heart of Toronto. The energy of Yonge-Dundas Square makes for an exciting, lively atmosphere.
- **Location:** 1 Dundas St E, Toronto, ON M5B 2R8
- **Cost:** Free
- **How to get there:** Take the **Line 1 subway** to **Dundas Station**.

5. Pedestrian Sundays in Kensington Market

Kensington Market (Spadina Ave & Dundas St W, Toronto, ON M5T 2E9) comes alive during **Pedestrian Sundays**, a monthly event where the streets are closed to cars, and the market transforms into a pedestrian-only space filled with live music, street performers, and local vendors. These events take place from May to October, and there's always free entertainment, from indie bands to world music.

- **Budget Tip:** Pedestrian Sundays are free, and since it's a community event, you can enjoy live music and street performances without spending anything. If you're hungry, grab a cheap bite at one of Kensington's many food stalls or restaurants, where meals typically cost **$10-15 CAD.**
- **Why it's perfect for budget travelers:** You get to experience Toronto's local culture in a vibrant, eclectic setting while enjoying free live performances. It's also a great way to explore Kensington Market, which is one of the city's most unique neighborhoods.
- **Location:** Spadina Ave & Dundas St W, Toronto, ON M5T 2E9
- **Cost:** Free
- **How to get there:** Take the **510 Spadina streetcar** to Kensington Market.

Indie Theaters and Cinemas with Discount Tickets.

1. TIFF Bell Lightbox

The **TIFF Bell Lightbox** (350 King St W, Toronto, ON M5V 3X5) is home to the **Toronto International Film Festival (TIFF)**, but it also operates year-round as a cinema that showcases indie films, documentaries, and international features. This is the place to go if you're a film buff looking for something off the beaten path.

- **Ticket Prices:** Regular tickets are **$15 CAD** for adults, but TIFF often offers **discounted matinees** before 5 PM, where tickets are priced at **$10-12 CAD.** There are also **membership options** that provide further discounts if you plan on visiting often.
- **Special Offers:** Keep an eye out for the **TIFF Next Wave Film Festival** in February, which offers **free screenings** for anyone under 25.

- **Why it's budget-friendly:** While it's not the cheapest theater, the Lightbox offers quality programming, and you're often paying less than you would for a mainstream blockbuster. The films shown here are also ones you might not see elsewhere.
- **Location:** TIFF Bell Lightbox, 350 King St W, Toronto, ON M5V 3X5
- **How to get there:** Take the **501 Queen** streetcar to **John Street**, or it's a short walk from **St. Andrew Station** on the **Line 1 subway**.

2. The Revue Cinema

The **Revue Cinema** (400 Roncesvalles Ave, Toronto, ON M6R 2M9) is one of Toronto's oldest independent theaters, operating since 1912. It's a neighborhood favorite located in the heart of **Roncesvalles Village**, known for showing indie films, cult classics, and documentaries at an affordable price.

- **Ticket Prices:** Regular admission is **$13 CAD**, but they offer **discounted matinee screenings** at **$9 CAD**. Seniors and students get an extra discount with tickets for **$9 CAD** at any time.
- **Special Events:** The Revue often hosts themed movie nights, such as **Drunken Cinema**, where tickets are around **$15 CAD** and include audience participation and fun activities.
- **Why it's budget-friendly:** The Revue's ticket prices are lower than many mainstream theaters, and their matinees are especially affordable. Plus, the cinema itself is a beautiful historic venue, so you're getting a cultural experience along with the film.
- **Location:** The Revue Cinema, 400 Roncesvalles Ave, Toronto, ON M6R 2M9
- **How to get there:** Take the **504 King streetcar** to Roncesvalles Ave and walk north to the theater.

3. Hot Docs Ted Rogers Cinema

NIGHTLIFE AND ENTERTAINMENT

For documentary lovers, the **Hot Docs Ted Rogers Cinema** (506 Bloor St W, Toronto, ON M5S 1Y3) is the place to be. This theater specializes in documentary films and frequently hosts **Hot Docs** screenings, as well as other indie and international films. It's a great option if you're looking for something more educational or thought-provoking.

- **Ticket Prices:** Regular tickets are **$15 CAD**, but they offer **$9 CAD matinee tickets** and discounted admission for seniors and students.
- **Special Offers:** During the annual **Hot Docs Festival**, there are special deals, and some screenings are offered on a **pay-what-you-can** basis.
- **Why it's budget-friendly:** With its matinee discounts and focus on documentaries, Hot Docs Ted Rogers Cinema offers a great value for film lovers. Plus, many of the documentaries are followed by Q&A sessions with the filmmakers, so you get more than just a movie.
- **Location:** Hot Docs Ted Rogers Cinema, 506 Bloor St W, Toronto, ON M5S 1Y3
- **How to get there:** Located right by **Bathurst Station** on the **Line 2 subway**.

4. **The Royal Cinema**

Another fantastic option for indie films and cult classics is **The Royal Cinema** (608 College St, Toronto, ON M6G 1B4). This theater often screens special events, retro films, and international movies that you won't find at mainstream theaters. They frequently host film festivals, Q&A events, and live performances as well.

- **Ticket Prices:** General admission is **$14 CAD**, but they offer **$12 CAD tickets** for students and seniors. Matinees and special screenings often have additional discounts.
- **Special Events:** The Royal regularly hosts **Toronto After Dark Film Festival**, which screens horror, sci-fi, and fantasy films, with tickets around **$15 CAD** for festival events.

- **Why it's budget-friendly:** The Royal has a great range of indie and cult films that you can't see anywhere else. They also offer discounts for students and often run special promotions for festival screenings.
- **Location:** The Royal Cinema, 608 College St, Toronto, ON M6G 1B4
- **How to get there:** Take the **506 Carlton streetcar** to **College St** and **Bathurst St**.

Budget-Friendly Nightclubs and Live Music Venues

1. The Horseshoe Tavern

One of Toronto's most iconic music venues, **The Horseshoe Tavern** (370 Queen St W, Toronto, ON M5V 2A2), has been hosting live bands since 1947. It's a must-visit for music lovers, and the best part is that many shows are either free or very cheap.

- **Cover Charge:** Depending on the night, cover charges can range from **free** to around **$10-15 CAD** for live bands. Monday nights often feature free or pay-what-you-can shows, making it a perfect spot for budget travelers.
- **Music Style:** The Horseshoe is known for showcasing a range of music genres, from rock and country to indie and folk. Many well-known Canadian bands, including **The Tragically Hip** and **Blue Rodeo**, got their start here.
- **Why it's budget-friendly:** The Horseshoe Tavern regularly features free shows and affordable cover charges for live music. Drinks here are also reasonably priced, with pints of local beer starting at **$7 CAD**.
- **Location:** The Horseshoe Tavern, 370 Queen St W, Toronto, ON M5V 2A2
- **How to get there:** Take the **501 Queen streetcar** to **Queen St W** and **Spadina Ave**.

NIGHTLIFE AND ENTERTAINMENT

2. The Drake Underground

If you're looking for a more modern vibe, **The Drake Underground** (1150 Queen St W, Toronto, ON M6J 1J3) is a trendy spot located in **The Drake Hotel**. It hosts live music, DJ nights, and indie bands, all at affordable prices.

- **Cover Charge:** On most nights, the cover charge is around **$10-20 CAD**, depending on the event. They also have **free shows** or pay-what-you-can events, especially during local artist showcases.
- **Music Style:** The Drake Underground features a mix of indie bands, electronic music, and up-and-coming artists. The venue is intimate, so it's a great spot to catch emerging talent before they make it big.
- **Why it's budget-friendly:** While the venue has a trendy feel, ticket prices are reasonable, and the shows are often affordable. Keep an eye on their calendar for free or discounted events.
- **Location:** The Drake Underground, 1150 Queen St W, Toronto, ON M6J 1J3
- **How to get there:** Take the **501 Queen streetcar** to **Queen St W** and **Dufferin St**.

3. Sneaky Dee's

Sneaky Dee's (431 College St, Toronto, ON M5T 1T1) is a Toronto institution that's part restaurant, part live music venue, and part nightclub. Known for its loud punk shows and cheap drinks, it's a favorite among locals for an affordable night out.

- **Cover Charge:** Most live shows have a cover charge between **$5-15 CAD**, depending on the band. On weekends, they often have DJ nights with no cover charge before **10 PM**.
- **Music Style:** You'll find a mix of punk, metal, rock, and indie bands playing at Sneaky Dee's. On DJ nights, expect a mix of pop, rock, and nostalgic hits from the 90s and 2000s.

- **Why it's budget-friendly:** The cover charges are low, and Sneaky Dee's also has some of the cheapest drinks in the city. Pints of beer start at **$6-7 CAD**, and their famous nachos are a great snack if you're looking for a late-night bite.
- **Location:** Sneaky Dee's, 431 College St, Toronto, ON M5T 1T1
- **How to get there:** Take the **506 Carlton streetcar** to **College St** and **Bathurst St**.

4. Bovine Sex Club

Despite its provocative name, **Bovine Sex Club** (542 Queen St W, Toronto, ON M5V 2B5) is one of Toronto's most beloved dive bars. It's a grungy, laid-back venue that's known for its live music, eclectic decor, and affordable drinks.

- **Cover Charge:** Cover is usually around **$10-15 CAD** for live shows. On some nights, there's no cover charge, especially if there's a local band playing.
- **Music Style:** Expect a mix of punk, rock, and alternative music, along with the occasional themed party or DJ night.
- **Why it's budget-friendly:** With low cover charges and affordable drinks, Bovine Sex Club is perfect for a fun night out that won't drain your wallet. It's a great place to hear live music without paying premium prices.
- **Location:** Bovine Sex Club, 542 Queen St W, Toronto, ON M5V 2B5
- **How to get there:** Take the **501 Queen streetcar** to **Queen St W** and **Bathurst St**.

5. Drom Taberna

For a more relaxed vibe with live music and Eastern European-inspired food, head to **Drom Taberna** (458 Queen St W, Toronto, ON M5V 2A8). This cozy venue features live bands playing everything from folk to jazz, with affordable cover charges and no-frills fun.

- **Cover Charge:** Most nights have a **pay-what-you-can** policy for live music, making it very budget-friendly. Some special events have a set cover charge, but it's usually no more than **$10 CAD**.
- **Music Style:** Expect a mix of folk, jazz, and Balkan-inspired music. Drom Taberna often hosts local musicians, giving it a unique, intimate feel.
- **Why it's budget-friendly:** With a pay-what-you-can policy and reasonably priced drinks and food, Drom Taberna offers a great value for a night out. It's a laid-back spot where you can enjoy good music and good company without spending a fortune.
- **Location:** Drom Taberna, 458 Queen St W, Toronto, ON M5V 2A8
- **How to get there:** Take the **501 Queen streetcar** to **Queen St W** and **Spadina Ave**.

Free and Low-Cost Evening Activities

1. Night Markets

Night markets in Toronto are a great way to experience the city's diverse food and culture in a lively atmosphere. They often feature a mix of food stalls, crafts, and live entertainment, giving you a chance to soak in the local vibe without spending too much.

The Toronto Night Market

- One of the most popular night markets in the city is the **Toronto Night Market**, typically held during the summer months in various locations, including **Scarborough** and **Markham**. The market showcases a wide range of street food from different cultures, along with local vendors selling crafts and goods. Admission is usually free, and you only pay for

what you want to eat or buy.
- **Budget Tip:** Go with friends and share dishes to try more food without spending too much. Most food items cost between **$5-10 CAD**.

Kensington Market Pedestrian Sundays

- While not strictly a night market, **Kensington Market Pedestrian Sundays** extend into the evening and offer a similar vibe. On the last Sunday of every month from May to October, the streets of Kensington Market are closed to cars, and the area transforms into a bustling market with street performances, food vendors, and live music. It's completely free to wander around, and you'll often find affordable food options from local vendors.
- **Location:** Kensington Market, Spadina Ave & Dundas St W
- **How to get there:** Take the **Spadina streetcar** to Kensington Market and explore the area on foot.
- **Cost:** Free to enter, food typically costs **$5-15 CAD**.

2. Public Art Exhibits and Murals

Toronto is home to a vibrant public art scene, and many exhibits and murals are free to enjoy, especially in the evening when they're beautifully lit. Walking through neighborhoods like **Queen Street West**, **The Distillery District**, or **Kensington Market**, you'll find colorful street art and murals that give the city its unique charm.

Graffiti Alley

- One of the best places to experience street art in Toronto is **Graffiti Alley**. This stretch of alleyway, located between **Spadina Avenue** and **Bathurst Street**, is covered in murals by local and international artists. It's free to visit, and the vibrant artwork looks particularly striking at

dusk.
- **Location:** Graffiti Alley, between Spadina Ave and Bathurst St, south of Queen St W
- **How to get there:** Take the **501 Queen streetcar** to Spadina Ave and walk south to the alley.
- **Cost:** Free.

The Bentway Art Exhibits

- The **Bentway** is a public space located under the **Gardiner Expressway** that frequently hosts free art installations and exhibits. During the warmer months, you'll find outdoor light shows and sculptures that are free to explore. In the winter, the area transforms into a free outdoor skating rink. The Bentway is open in the evenings, so it's a perfect spot for a low-cost night out.
- **Location:** 250 Fort York Blvd, Toronto, ON M5V 3K9
- **How to get there:** Take the **511 Bathurst streetcar** or the **509 Harbourfront streetcar** to Fort York Blvd.
- **Cost:** Free to explore art exhibits; skate rentals are available for a fee during the winter season.

3. **Light Shows and Installations**

Throughout the year, Toronto hosts several free or low-cost light shows that brighten up the evening hours. These events are especially popular during the winter months, but you can also find some during the summer.

Cavalcade of Lights

- Every year, **Nathan Phillips Square** becomes the site of the **Cavalcade of Lights**, a festive light show that kicks off the holiday season. The event usually starts in late November and includes a tree-lighting ceremony,

live music performances, and an ice-skating rink that's free to use if you bring your own skates (rentals are available for **$10-15 CAD**). The square is lit up with thousands of twinkling lights, making it a magical place to visit after dark.
- **Location:** Nathan Phillips Square, 100 Queen St W, Toronto, ON M5H 2N1
- **How to get there:** Take the **Queen streetcar** to **Bay St** or the **Line 1 subway** to **Queen Station**.
- **Cost:** Free to attend; skate rentals available for a fee.

Toronto Light Festival (Distillery District)

- The **Toronto Light Festival** takes place in the Distillery District each winter, turning the historic area into a glowing wonderland of light installations. It's free to wander around and admire the creative, illuminated artwork. The festival runs from January to March and offers a perfect way to spend an evening exploring the city without spending much.
- **Location:** Distillery District, 55 Mill St, Toronto, ON M5A 3C4
- **How to get there:** Take the **504 King streetcar** to the **Distillery Loop**.
- **Cost:** Free.

4. Live Music and Performances

Toronto is a hub for live music, and you don't need to spend a lot to enjoy a great performance. There are several venues around the city that host free or low-cost live music in the evenings, especially during the summer months when outdoor concerts are popular.

Harbourfront Centre

- During the summer, **Harbourfront Centre** (235 Queens Quay W,

NIGHTLIFE AND ENTERTAINMENT

Toronto, ON M5J 2G8) hosts free concerts and cultural performances as part of their **Summer Music in the Garden** series. These performances take place at **Toronto Music Garden**, an outdoor space along the waterfront. You can bring a blanket, sit back, and enjoy live music in a beautiful setting—completely free.

- **Location:** 235 Queens Quay W, Toronto, ON M5J 2G8
- **How to get there:** Take the **509 Harbourfront streetcar** to **Queens Quay W**.
- **Cost:** Free.

The Rex Hotel Jazz & Blues Bar

- For low-cost live music indoors, head to **The Rex Hotel Jazz & Blues Bar** (194 Queen St W, Toronto, ON M5V 1Z1), where you can catch jazz performances every night of the week. The cover charge is usually around **$10-15 CAD**, making it an affordable option for an evening of entertainment. Plus, the intimate setting and talented performers make it one of the best spots in Toronto for live music on a budget.
- **Location:** 194 Queen St W, Toronto, ON M5V 1Z1
- **How to get there:** Take the **501 Queen streetcar** to **Queen St W and University Ave**.
- **Cost:** Cover charge is typically **$10-15 CAD**.

5. Outdoor Movie Nights

During the summer months, several parks and public spaces in Toronto offer free outdoor movie screenings. These events are perfect for a laid-back evening, where you can enjoy classic films or new releases under the stars.

Sail-In Cinema (Sugar Beach)

- One of the most unique outdoor movie experiences in Toronto is **Sail-In**

Cinema at **Sugar Beach**. Held in August, this free event shows movies on a giant floating screen, and you can either watch from the shore or, if you're lucky, from a boat. It's a great way to spend an evening by the waterfront without spending a dime.
- **Location:** Sugar Beach, 25 Dockside Dr, Toronto, ON M5A 0B5
- **How to get there:** Take the **6 Bay bus** to **Queens Quay East**.
- **Cost:** Free.

Christie Pits Film Festival

- Another popular outdoor movie series is the **Christie Pits Film Festival**, which runs from June to August at **Christie Pits Park**. The screenings are free, although donations are welcome. The festival often features a mix of classic films and recent releases, and you can bring your own blanket and snacks for a cozy movie night in the park.
- **Location:** Christie Pits Park, 750 Bloor St W, Toronto, ON M6G 3K4
- **How to get there:** Take the **Line 2 subway** to **Christie Station**.
- **Cost:** Free, with optional donations.

6. **Art Gallery of Ontario (AGO) – Free Wednesday Evenings**

If you're a fan of art, don't miss the chance to visit the **Art Gallery of Ontario (AGO)** (317 Dundas St W, Toronto, ON M5T 1G4) for free on Wednesday evenings. From **6:00 PM to 9:00 PM**, admission to the AGO's permanent collections is free, giving you the chance to explore works by Canadian and international artists without paying the usual **$25 CAD** admission fee.

- **Location:** 317 Dundas St W, Toronto, ON M5T 1G4
- **How to get there:** Take the **505 Dundas streetcar** to **McCaul St**.
- **Cost:** Free on Wednesdays from **6:00 PM to 9:00 PM**.

Day Trips on a Budget

Day Trips from Toronto: Niagara Falls, Hamilton, and More

1. **Niagara Falls**

One of the most popular day trips from Toronto is a visit to **Niagara Falls**, just under two hours away. The Falls are breathtaking, and there's plenty to see and do without spending a lot of money. The best part? You can easily make the trip on a budget using public transportation.

What to do in Niagara Falls on a budget:

- Start by walking along the **Niagara Parkway** to get the best views of the falls for free. The main observation points, such as **Table Rock Welcome Centre** (6650 Niagara Parkway, Niagara Falls, ON L2E 6T2), are completely free and offer stunning views of both the American and Horseshoe Falls. If you're interested in learning more about the falls, check out the free **Niagara Falls History Museum**.

Budget Tip: Skip the expensive boat tours if you're trying to save. While the **Hornblower Cruises** are an exciting way to get close to the falls, they cost around **$35 CAD**. Instead, take a stroll to the bottom of the falls and feel the mist for free at **Journey Behind the Falls**, which is **$23 CAD**.

- **How to get there:** Take the **GO Train** or **GO Bus** from **Union Station** to **Niagara Falls**. A round-trip fare on the **GO Train** is around **$25 CAD** for adults. Alternatively, buses such as **Megabus** or **Greyhound** offer round-trip tickets starting at **$20-30 CAD**.

- **Location:** Niagara Falls, ON L2E 6T2
- **Cost:** Free to walk along the falls; optional paid attractions
- **How to get there:** From Union Station, take the **GO Train** or **GO Bus** to **Niagara Falls**. The trip takes about 2 hours, and a round-trip ticket costs **$25 CAD**.

2. **Hamilton**

Hamilton is another great day trip destination that's affordable and close to Toronto. Known as the "City of Waterfalls," Hamilton is home to more than 100 waterfalls, many of which are free to visit and perfect for nature lovers.

What to do in Hamilton on a budget:

- Visit **Webster's Falls** and **Tews Falls**, two of Hamilton's most famous waterfalls. These spots are located in **Spencer Gorge Conservation Area**, and while parking costs around **$10 CAD**, there's no fee to visit the falls themselves. For more free activities, take a walk through **Bayfront Park** for scenic views of **Hamilton Harbour**.

Budget Tip: Pack a picnic and enjoy it at **Dundurn Castle Park**, which offers free entry to its grounds. You can also visit the nearby **Royal Botanical Gardens** (entry is **$10 CAD**) if you're interested in exploring more of Hamilton's natural beauty.

- **How to get there:** The easiest and cheapest way to get to Hamilton is by **GO Train** or **GO Bus**. The trip takes about an hour from **Union Station**, and a round-trip ticket costs **$18 CAD**. Alternatively, **Greyhound** buses

offer tickets starting around **$10-15 CAD** each way.
- **Location:** Hamilton, ON
- **Cost:** Free to visit waterfalls; parking costs around **$10 CAD**
- **How to get there:** Take the **GO Train** or **GO Bus** from Union Station to Hamilton. Round-trip fare is **$18 CAD**.

3. **Elora Gorge**

For a peaceful day away from the city, visit **Elora Gorge**, about an hour and a half northwest of Toronto. This scenic spot is perfect for hiking, picnicking, and even tubing down the **Grand River** in the summer months.

What to do in Elora Gorge on a budget:

- You can hike along the gorge and explore the nearby **Elora Quarry Conservation Area**. There is a small entry fee to enter the conservation area, which costs around **$6 CAD** for adults, but the scenic views and peaceful atmosphere make it well worth the price.

Budget Tip: Pack your own lunch to avoid spending money on food. The charming **Elora Village** nearby is fun to explore, with many free art galleries and affordable cafes. You can get a coffee for around **$2-3 CAD** at local spots like **The Lost & Found Café**.

- **How to get there:** While there's no direct **GO Train** to Elora, you can take a **Greyhound bus** or **Megabus** from **Union Station** to **Guelph** for around **$15-20 CAD** and then catch a local bus or taxi to Elora.
- **Location:** Elora, ON N0B 1S0
- **Cost:** **$6 CAD** for entry to Elora Gorge; free to explore the village
- **How to get there:** Take a **Greyhound** or **Megabus** to **Guelph** and transfer to a local bus or taxi to Elora. Bus tickets are around **$15-20 CAD** each way.

4. Prince Edward County

For a more laid-back day trip, head to **Prince Edward County**, known for its beautiful wineries, beaches, and charming small towns. While wineries might sound expensive, there are plenty of ways to enjoy the area on a budget.

What to do in Prince Edward County on a budget:

- Spend the day at **Sandbanks Provincial Park**, home to some of Ontario's best beaches. Entry to the park costs **$15 CAD** per vehicle, and you can spend the whole day swimming, sunbathing, and exploring the sand dunes. Another option is to visit **Picton**, the largest town in the county, where you can explore local shops and galleries for free.

Budget Tip: If you want to try some wine but don't want to break the bank, visit smaller wineries like **Huff Estates** or **Casa Dea Estates**, which often offer affordable tastings for around **$5-10 CAD**.

- **How to get there:** You'll need to rent a car to get to Prince Edward County, as there's no direct public transportation. Car rentals in Toronto can cost around **$50-80 CAD** for the day, making it an affordable option if you're traveling with friends and can split the cost.
- **Location:** Prince Edward County, ON
- **Cost:** $15 CAD per vehicle to enter Sandbanks Provincial Park; wine tastings start at **$5 CAD**
- **How to get there:** Rent a car from Toronto and drive to Prince Edward County. Car rentals start at **$50-80 CAD** per day.

5. Blue Mountain

Located about two hours north of Toronto, **Blue Mountain** is a popular year-round destination for both adventure seekers and those looking to relax. In the winter, it's known for skiing, but during the warmer months, it offers hiking trails, scenic gondola rides, and free outdoor events.

What to do in Blue Mountain on a budget:

- During the summer and fall, you can hike many of the trails around **Blue Mountain Village** for free. The scenic views of **Georgian Bay** are stunning, especially if you hike up to **Scenic Caves Nature Adventures**, which costs **$10 CAD** for access to the caves and suspension bridge.

Budget Tip: If you're visiting during the summer, take advantage of the free outdoor concerts and events that Blue Mountain Village hosts. Pack a lunch and enjoy a picnic by the water to keep costs down.

- **How to get there:** The easiest way to get to Blue Mountain is by renting a car, which costs about **$50-80 CAD** for the day. Alternatively, you can take a **Greyhound bus** to **Collingwood** and then a local bus or taxi to Blue Mountain, with round-trip tickets costing around **$25-35 CAD**.
- **Location:** Blue Mountain, ON
- **Cost:** Free to hike; Scenic Caves entry is **$10 CAD**
- **How to get there:** Rent a car or take a **Greyhound bus** to Collingwood and transfer to Blue Mountain. Bus tickets are **$25-35 CAD** round-trip.

Affordable Transportation for Day Trips: GO Trains and Buses

If you're planning a day trip from Toronto, **GO Transit** offers one of the most affordable and convenient ways to get to nearby destinations. The **GO Train** and **GO Bus** networks connect Toronto to cities like Niagara Falls, Hamilton, and Guelph, making it easy to explore Ontario without needing to rent a car.

1. **Using GO Trains for Budget Day Trips**

GO Trains are a comfortable and budget-friendly way to travel around southern Ontario. The trains depart from **Union Station** in downtown Toronto and connect to many of the top day trip destinations.

How to use the GO Train:

- To travel on the GO Train, you'll need to purchase a **Presto card** or buy a one-time ticket from a machine at the station. A Presto card is ideal if you're planning multiple trips, as it offers discounted fares. You can purchase one at **Union Station** for **$6 CAD** and load it with funds for your trip.

Ticket costs:

- **Niagara Falls:** Round-trip fare is around **$25 CAD** for adults.
- **Hamilton:** Round-trip fare is **$18 CAD** for adults.
- **Guelph:** Round-trip fare is about **$20 CAD**.

Best routes:

- For Niagara Falls, take the **Lakeshore West line** from **Union Station** to **Niagara Falls Station**. The trip takes about 2 hours.
- For Hamilton, take the **Lakeshore West line** to **Hamilton GO Centre**, which takes about an hour.
- For Guelph, take the **Kitchener line** to **Guelph Central Station**. The trip takes around 90 minutes.

2. **Using Buses for Budget Day Trips**

Buses are another affordable option for day trips, especially if your destination isn't directly served by the GO Train. Companies like **Greyhound** and **Megabus** operate routes from Toronto to nearby cities and towns, often at lower prices than the GO Train.

How to use the bus:

- You can book tickets online or buy them at the station. Megabus and Greyhound both offer flexible cancellation policies, making them a good option if your plans change.

Ticket costs:

- **Niagara Falls: $20-30 CAD** round-trip on Greyhound or Megabus.
- **Hamilton: $10-15 CAD** each way on Greyhound.
- **Collingwood/Blue Mountain: $25-35 CAD** round-trip.

Best routes:

- For Niagara Falls, both **Greyhound** and **Megabus** offer frequent trips from **Toronto Coach Terminal** (610 Bay St).
- For Hamilton, take a **Greyhound** bus from **Union Station** or **Toronto Coach Terminal**. The trip takes about an hour.
- For Collingwood, take a **Greyhound** bus to **Collingwood** and then transfer to a local bus or taxi to reach **Blue Mountain**.

Budget-Friendly Nature Escapes: Hiking Trails and Parks

1. High Park

One of the largest parks in Toronto, **High Park** (1873 Bloor St W, Toronto, ON M6R 2Z3) is a perfect spot for a budget-friendly day of hiking, picnicking, and exploring nature. The park features over 400 acres of greenery, including trails, ponds, and even a small zoo that's free to visit.

- **Hiking Trails:** High Park has several well-maintained walking trails that are easy to navigate. You can explore the **Grenadier Pond** area for a peaceful walk around the water, or hike up to **Hillside Gardens** for scenic views of the park's cherry blossoms in spring.
- **Cost:** Free to enter. There's no admission fee for the park or the zoo.

Budget Tip: Bring your own snacks or a picnic to enjoy at one of the many picnic areas scattered throughout the park. This will help you avoid the higher prices at nearby cafes.

- **Location:** High Park, 1873 Bloor St W, Toronto, ON M6R 2Z3
- **How to get there:** Take the **Line 2 subway** to **High Park Station** and walk south into the park.
- **Cost:** Free

2. **Scarborough Bluffs**

For a stunning view of Lake Ontario and a relaxing day in nature, head to the **Scarborough Bluffs** (1 Brimley Rd S, Toronto, ON M1M 1T9). The Bluffs stretch for nearly 15 kilometers along the lake, offering spectacular cliffs, sandy beaches, and plenty of walking trails. It's a perfect spot for budget travelers looking for a nature escape without leaving the city.

- **Hiking Trails:** The **Bluffer's Park Trail** is a popular route that takes you along the waterfront and offers beautiful views of the cliffs. It's an easy walk, making it great for casual hikers and families.
- **Cost:** Free to enter. There's no admission fee for the Bluffs or the trails.

Budget Tip: Parking can be expensive during peak times, so consider taking the TTC or biking to avoid parking fees.

- **Location:** Scarborough Bluffs 1 Brimley Rd S, Toronto, ON M1M 1T9
- **How to get there:** Take the **12 Kingston Rd bus** from **Kennedy**

Station to **Brimley Rd South**.
- **Cost:** Free

3. **Rouge National Urban Park**

Rouge National Urban Park (1749 Meadowvale Rd, Toronto, ON M1B 5W8) is Canada's first national urban park, and it's an excellent option for budget travelers looking to hike, camp, or enjoy a day in nature. The park spans over 79 square kilometers and offers a mix of forests, wetlands, and meadows, making it one of the most diverse green spaces near the city.

- **Hiking Trails:** Rouge Park has several well-marked trails for all skill levels. The **Vista Trail** is a 1.5-kilometer loop that offers great views of the surrounding forests, while the **Mast Trail** is a longer 4.5-kilometer trail that takes you through lush greenery and along the Rouge River.
- **Cost:** Free to enter. There's no fee for hiking, and parking is free in designated lots.

Budget Tip: Pack a picnic and enjoy it at one of the park's designated picnic areas. The park also has several free camping spots, but you'll need to reserve in advance through the **Parks Canada** website.

- **Location:** Rouge National Urban Park 1749 Meadowvale Rd, Toronto, ON M1B 5W8
- **How to get there:** Take the **85 Sheppard East bus** from **Don Mills Station** to **Meadowvale Rd**.
- **Cost:** Free

4. **The Don Valley Trails**

The **Don Valley** is home to several scenic trails that run along the Don River, offering budget-friendly hiking and biking opportunities. The trails wind through forests and wetlands, providing a peaceful escape from the city without requiring much travel.

- **Hiking Trails:** The **Lower Don Trail** is a 6.8-kilometer path that runs along the Don River, connecting several parks and green spaces. It's perfect for a relaxing walk or bike ride, with plenty of benches and rest spots along the way.
- **Cost:** Free to enter and explore. You can bring your own bike or rent one for the day if you prefer cycling over walking.

Budget Tip: If you don't have your own bike, you can use **Bike Share Toronto**, which has stations along the Don Valley. Renting a bike costs **$3.25 CAD for 30 minutes** or **$7 CAD for a day pass**.

- **Location:** Don Valley Trails Various entry points along the Don River
- **How to get there:** Take the **Line 2 subway** to **Broadview Station** and walk or bike down into the valley.
- **Cost:** Free

5. Glen Stewart Ravine

If you're looking for a quiet, hidden gem within the city, **Glen Stewart Ravine** (351 Glen Manor Dr, Toronto, ON M4E 2X9) is a perfect choice. This small but beautiful ravine offers peaceful walking trails and a chance to escape the hustle and bustle of downtown Toronto.

- **Hiking Trails:** The **Glen Stewart Trail** is a short 1.2-kilometer loop that takes you through a forested ravine and alongside a small creek. It's a great spot for a relaxing walk, especially in the fall when the leaves change color.
- **Cost:** Free to enter.

Budget Tip: Glen Stewart Ravine is close to the **Beaches** neighborhood, where you can end your hike with a budget-friendly meal or coffee at one of the local cafes.

- **Location:** Glen Stewart Ravine, 351 Glen Manor Dr, Toronto, ON M4E 2X9
- **How to get there:** Take the **501 Queen streetcar** to **Glen Manor Dr**.
- **Cost:** Free

Nearby Small Towns Worth Visiting on a Budget

1. Niagara-on-the-Lake

Located about an hour and a half from Toronto, **Niagara-on-the-Lake** is a picturesque town known for its well-preserved 19th-century architecture, boutique shops, and wineries. While it's often associated with wine tours, there are plenty of free or low-cost activities to enjoy.

Budget Tip: Stroll through the town's historic **Queen Street** and admire the beautifully preserved buildings. Many of the shops have unique, affordable souvenirs, and window shopping is free. You can also visit **Fort George**, a historic site from the War of 1812, where admission is around **$12 CAD** for adults.

- **How to get there:** You can take the **Go Transit** bus from **Union Station** to **Niagara Falls**, and then a local bus or taxi to Niagara-on-the-Lake. The **Go Transit weekend day pass** costs around **$10-15 CAD**.
- **Location:** Niagara-on-the-Lake, ON
- **Cost:** Free to explore the town; Fort George entry **$12 CAD**
- **How to get there:** Go Transit bus or car

2. Elora

Elora is a charming small town about an hour and a half drive from

Toronto, known for its stunning natural landscapes, including the **Elora Gorge** and **Elora Quarry**. It's an ideal destination for budget travelers who enjoy hiking, swimming, or exploring quaint villages.

Budget Tip: The **Elora Gorge Conservation Area** offers affordable admission (around **$7 CAD** per person) and features hiking trails along the gorge, as well as picnic areas. If you visit in the summer, the **Elora Quarry** is a popular swimming spot, and entry is also about **$7 CAD**.

- **How to get there:** Elora is best reached by car, but you can take a **Go Transit bus** to **Guelph**, followed by a local bus to Elora.
- **Location:** Elora, ON
- **Cost:** Elora Gorge entry **$7 CAD**
- **How to get there:** Go Transit or car

3. Port Perry

For a peaceful day by the lake, head to **Port Perry**, a small town located about an hour northeast of Toronto. Port Perry sits on the shores of **Lake Scugog** and offers beautiful views, quaint shops, and plenty of affordable outdoor activities.

Budget Tip: Stroll along the **Port Perry Marina** and enjoy the views of the lake. You can also visit **Palmer Park**, which has a lovely walking trail and picnic areas. If you're into local history, stop by the **Scugog Shores Museum** for a small admission fee of **$5 CAD**.

- **How to get there:** You can reach Port Perry by car, or take the **Go Transit** bus to **Whitby** and then a local bus to Port Perry.
- **Location:** Port Perry, ON
- **Cost:** Free to explore the town; Scugog Shores Museum entry **$5 CAD**
- **How to get there:** Go Transit or car

4. St. Jacobs

St. Jacobs is a small town located about an hour and a half from Toronto, known for its Mennonite community, farmers' market, and quaint shops. It's a great destination for a budget-friendly day trip, especially if you enjoy exploring small towns with a strong sense of history and tradition.

- **Budget Tip:** Visit the **St. Jacobs Farmers' Market**, which is one of the largest year-round farmers' markets in Ontario. You can sample local foods, buy affordable produce, and browse handmade crafts. Entry to the market is free, and there are plenty of budget-friendly snacks available for **$5-10 CAD**.
- **How to get there:** You can take the **Go Transit bus** to **Kitchener** and then a local bus or taxi to St. Jacobs.
- **Location:** St. Jacobs, ON
- **Cost:** Free to explore; Farmers' Market is free to enter
- **How to get there:** Go Transit or car

5. Unionville

Closer to Toronto, **Unionville** is a historic village in **Markham** that's full of charm. It's a quick and affordable day trip destination, just a 30-minute drive from downtown Toronto. Unionville's **Main Street** is lined with well-preserved 19th-century buildings, cafes, and shops, making it a perfect spot for a leisurely stroll.

- **Budget Tip:** Take a walk along **Toogood Pond** for a relaxing escape from the city. There's no admission fee, and the surrounding park is perfect for a picnic. You can also visit the **Varley Art Gallery** for free.
- **How to get there:** Unionville is easily accessible by **Go Transit** from Union Station, with a round-trip fare costing around **$10 CAD**.
- **Location:** Unionville, ON
- **Cost:** Free to explore
- **How to get there:** Go Transit or car.

Budget Itineraries

1-Day Budget Itinerary: Exploring Toronto on Foot

This one-day walking itinerary is perfect for budget travelers who want to see Toronto's top attractions without spending too much. By focusing on free sights and affordable food options, you'll get a full experience of the city's highlights while keeping costs low.

Morning

Start at Union Station

Begin your day at **Union Station** (65 Front St W, Toronto, ON M5J 1E6), Toronto's central transportation hub and a stunning architectural landmark. You can take in the impressive design of the station's Great Hall, which dates back to 1927, for free.

Walk to Nathan Phillips Square

From Union Station, walk north on Bay Street for about 10 minutes to **Nathan Phillips Square** (100 Queen St W, Toronto, ON M5H 2N1). This public square is home to the iconic **Toronto Sign** and **City Hall**. It's a great place to take photos and people-watch. If you're visiting during the winter, you can skate here for free if you bring your own skates (rentals cost about **$10-15 CAD**).

Explore Graffiti Alley

BUDGET ITINERARIES

Next, head west on Queen Street West to **Graffiti Alley** (Queen St W & Portland St, Toronto, ON M5V 2L7). This colorful stretch of alleyway is covered in murals and street art and is a must-see for art lovers. The best part? It's completely free to wander and take photos. The alley runs parallel to Queen Street and spans several blocks, so take your time exploring the vibrant art.

Lunch
Lunch at Kensington Market

Continue walking west along Queen Street West and then head north to **Kensington Market** (Spadina Ave & Dundas St W, Toronto, ON M5T 2E9). This eclectic neighborhood is full of affordable food options, ranging from international street food to vegan treats. For a budget-friendly meal, try **Seven Lives Tacos** (69 Kensington Ave) where you can get a delicious taco for around **$7-10 CAD**. The market is also a great place to explore vintage shops and street vendors.

Afternoon
Visit the Art Gallery of Ontario (AGO)

After lunch, walk a few blocks east to the **Art Gallery of Ontario (AGO)** (317 Dundas St W, Toronto, ON M5T 1G4). The AGO is free on Wednesday evenings from **6:00 PM to 9:00 PM**, but if you're visiting during the day, admission is around **$25 CAD**. If you're on a strict budget, you can admire the building's architecture from the outside and continue walking.

Stroll Through Queen's Park

Next, head north to **Queen's Park** (111 Wellesley St W, Toronto, ON M7A 1A1), a beautiful green space that surrounds the Ontario Legislative Building. Take a peaceful walk through the park's tree-lined paths, and if you're interested, you can take a free self-guided tour of the **Ontario Legislature**.

Evening

Dinner in Chinatown

End your day by heading back south to **Chinatown** (Spadina Ave & Dundas St W), where you'll find plenty of budget-friendly dining options. Stop at **Mother's Dumplings** (421 Spadina Ave), where you can get a plate of handmade dumplings for about **$8-12 CAD**. It's a great way to end the day with a warm, affordable meal.

Optional Evening Activity: Harbourfront Stroll

If you have the energy, finish your evening with a stroll along the **Toronto Harbourfront**. From Chinatown, walk south on Spadina Avenue toward **Harbourfront Centre** (235 Queens Quay W). The waterfront offers beautiful views of Lake Ontario and the CN Tower lit up at night. This peaceful walk is completely free and a relaxing way to end your day.

3-Day Budget Itinerary: Top Attractions and Free Activities

For those staying a little longer, this three-day itinerary will take you through Toronto's major sights, free activities, and budget-friendly food options. Each day is planned to help you maximize value while seeing the best of what Toronto has to offer.

Day 1: Downtown and Harbourfront
  Morning:
  Start at St. Lawrence Market

Begin your day at **St. Lawrence Market** (93 Front St E, Toronto, ON M5E 1C3), one of Toronto's oldest and most famous markets. While the market is free to explore, you can grab a budget-friendly breakfast at one of the vendors. Try the iconic **peameal bacon sandwich** for around **$7-10 CAD**.

Walk to the Distillery District

From St. Lawrence Market, walk east to the **Distillery District** (55 Mill St, Toronto, ON M5A 3C4). This pedestrian-only area is known for its cobblestone streets and historic buildings. While many of the shops and galleries are on the pricier side, simply walking through the district and admiring the architecture is free.

Lunch:

Lunch at a Food Truck

For a budget-friendly lunch, head back toward downtown and grab a bite from one of Toronto's many food trucks. You can often find trucks around **Nathan Phillips Square** or the Harbourfront, offering everything from hot dogs to gourmet tacos for around **$5-10 CAD**.

Afternoon:

Visit the CN Tower (Outside)

While entry to the **CN Tower** (301 Front St W, Toronto, ON M5V 2T6) is around **$43 CAD**, you can still enjoy its grandeur from the outside. Walk around the base of the tower and take in the views of the surrounding area, including **Rogers Centre** and **Ripley's Aquarium**.

Explore Harbourfront Centre

After admiring the CN Tower, head south to **Harbourfront Centre** (235 Queens Quay W). This area offers free art exhibits, outdoor performances, and beautiful views of Lake Ontario. In the summer, you can catch free concerts or outdoor movie screenings, while in the winter, the area transforms into an outdoor skating rink.

Dinner:

Dinner at The Rex Hotel Jazz & Blues Bar

End your first day with dinner and live music at **The Rex Hotel Jazz & Blues Bar** (194 Queen St W, Toronto, ON M5V 1Z1). The cover charge is usually **$10-15 CAD**, and the menu includes affordable options like burgers and sandwiches for around **$10-15 CAD**.

Day 2: Parks and Culture

Morning:

Visit High Park

Start your second day at **High Park** (1873 Bloor St W, Toronto, ON M6R 2Z3), one of Toronto's largest green spaces. Spend your morning exploring the park's walking trails, visiting the free zoo, and enjoying the peaceful surroundings. The cherry blossoms in spring are a must-see if you're visiting at that time of year.

Lunch:

Picnic in High Park

Pack a picnic or grab something affordable from a nearby grocery store or cafe before heading into the park. This is a great way to save money while enjoying the scenery.

Afternoon:

Visit the Royal Ontario Museum (Free Wednesday Evenings)

In the afternoon, make your way to the **Royal Ontario Museum (ROM)** (100 Queens Park, Toronto, ON M5S 2C6). If you're visiting on a Wednesday, admission is free from **5:30 PM to 8:30 PM**. Otherwise, admission is around **$23 CAD** for adults. The ROM offers a fascinating look at natural history, art, and culture from around the world.

Stroll Through Yorkville

After visiting the ROM, take a walk through **Yorkville**, Toronto's upscale shopping district. While the stores can be pricey, window shopping is free, and the area is full of art galleries, beautiful architecture, and charming streets.

Dinner:

Affordable Dinner in Koreatown

End your day with a budget-friendly dinner in **Koreatown** (Bloor St W & Christie St). This neighborhood is known for its affordable, delicious

Korean food. Try **Buk Chang Dong Soon Tofu** (691 Bloor St W), where you can get a hearty tofu soup for around **$10-12 CAD**.

Day 3: Art and Local Neighborhoods
Morning:
Explore Kensington Market and Chinatown

Begin your final day in **Kensington Market** (Spadina Ave & Dundas St W, Toronto, ON M5T 2E9). Spend the morning browsing vintage shops, sampling street food, and exploring the eclectic mix of art, murals, and local vendors. It's a budget traveler's dream, with affordable eats and unique finds. Afterward, walk over to **Chinatown** and explore the shops along **Spadina Avenue**.

Lunch:
Lunch at Mother's Dumplings

For a cheap and filling meal, head to **Mother's Dumplings** (421 Spadina Ave). A plate of dumplings costs around **$8-12 CAD**, making it an affordable lunch option in Chinatown.

Afternoon:
Free Art at the Distillery District

In the afternoon, head back to the **Distillery District** for a second visit if you haven't fully explored it. This time, focus on the free public art installations scattered throughout the district. It's a relaxing way to spend an afternoon, and you can enjoy the historic charm without spending money.

Visit The Bentway

If you have more time, visit **The Bentway** (250 Fort York Blvd), a public space located under the Gardiner Expressway. The area frequently hosts free art exhibits, performances, and outdoor events, making it a great budget-friendly stop.

Dinner:

Dinner at a Local Pub

For your last meal in Toronto, enjoy a budget-friendly dinner at one of the city's many local pubs. Head to **Sneaky Dee's** (431 College St), a Toronto institution known for its cheap eats and lively atmosphere. You can get a filling plate of nachos or a burger for around **$10-15 CAD**, making it an affordable way to cap off your three-day trip.

5-Day Itinerary: A Full Week of Budget-Friendly Adventures

Day 1: Explore the Heart of Downtown Toronto

Start your adventure by diving into the heart of Toronto's downtown core. It's a great way to get familiar with the city, and you can do much of it for free or very little cost.

Morning: Stroll Through Nathan Phillips Square

Start your day at **Nathan Phillips Square** (100 Queen St W, Toronto, ON M5H 2N1), a central public space that's home to the iconic **Toronto sign** and City Hall. It's free to explore, and if you visit during the winter, there's a free skating rink (bring your own skates or rent for **$10-15 CAD**).

- **Location:** Nathan Phillips Square, 100 Queen St W, Toronto
- **Cost:** Free, skate rentals are optional
- **How to get there:** Take the **Line 1 subway** to **Queen Station**.

Midday: Visit the Art Gallery of Ontario (AGO)

- Head over to the **Art Gallery of Ontario** (317 Dundas St W, Toronto, ON M5T 1G4), where you can visit for free on Wednesday evenings from **6:00 PM to 9:00 PM**. The AGO houses a vast collection of Canadian and international art, and even if you're not there on a free day, tickets are reasonably priced at **$25 CAD**.

- **Cost:** Free on Wednesday evenings, regular admission **$25 CAD**
- **How to get there:** Take the **505 Dundas streetcar** to McCaul St.

Afternoon: Walk Through Kensington Market

Spend the afternoon exploring **Kensington Market** (Spadina Ave & Dundas St W), one of Toronto's most vibrant and eclectic neighborhoods. This is a great spot for window shopping, people-watching, and grabbing a cheap bite to eat. You'll find plenty of budget-friendly restaurants and food stalls offering everything from tacos to Jamaican patties for **$5-10 CAD**. Don't miss the vintage shops and street art that give this neighborhood its character.

- **Cost:** Free to explore, meals for **$5-10 CAD**
- **How to get there:** Take the **Spadina streetcar** to Kensington Market.

Evening: Catch the Sunset at Harbourfront

- End your day with a walk along the **Harbourfront** (235 Queens Quay W, Toronto, ON M5J 2G8), where you can enjoy free public art installations, live performances, and beautiful views of **Lake Ontario**. Grab a bench or bring a blanket and watch the sun set over the water for free. If you're here in the summer, look out for free concerts and cultural events hosted at **Harbourfront Centre**.
- **Cost:** Free
- **How to get there:** Take the **509 Harbourfront streetcar** to Queens Quay W.

Day 2: Outdoor Adventures and Nature

Toronto is surrounded by natural beauty, and you can spend a day hiking, exploring parks, and relaxing by the water—all without spending much.

Morning: Hike at High Park

Spend the morning at **High Park** (1873 Bloor St W), one of the largest parks in the city. The park offers plenty of hiking trails, beautiful gardens, and even a small zoo that's free to visit. You can easily spend a few hours here exploring the trails around **Grenadier Pond**, the cherry blossoms in spring, or the fall colors later in the year.

- **Cost:** Free
- **How to get there:** Take the **Line 2 subway** to **High Park Station**.

Afternoon: Visit the Beaches

Head to the **Beaches** neighborhood for a relaxing afternoon by the water. You can stroll along **Woodbine Beach**, swim in **Lake Ontario**, or walk the **Boardwalk** for beautiful views of the city's shoreline. Pack a picnic to enjoy at one of the park's picnic areas, or grab an affordable snack from one of the nearby food trucks.

- **Cost:** Free
- **How to get there:** Take the **501 Queen streetcar** east to **Woodbine Ave**.

Evening: Sunset at the Scarborough Bluffs

- End your day at the **Scarborough Bluffs** (1 Brimley Rd S), one of the most scenic spots in Toronto. The **Bluffer's Park Trail** offers stunning views of the cliffs and Lake Ontario, and it's a perfect place to catch the sunset. Bring your camera—it's one of the best free activities in the city.
- **Cost:** Free
- **How to get there:** Take the **12 Kingston Rd bus** from **Kennedy Station** to **Brimley Rd South**.

Day 3: Culture and History

Spend a day exploring Toronto's rich cultural and historical landmarks, all while staying within your budget.

Morning: Discover the Distillery District

Start your day with a walk through the **Distillery District** (55 Mill St), a historic pedestrian-only area with beautifully preserved Victorian-era industrial architecture. It's free to wander the cobblestone streets and explore the many art galleries, shops, and public art installations. If you're visiting in the winter, the **Toronto Christmas Market** is a must-see, and entrance is free on weekdays.

- **Cost:** Free
- **How to get there:** Take the **504 King streetcar** to the **Distillery Loop**.
- **Midday: Visit St. Lawrence Market**
- Head over to **St. Lawrence Market** (93 Front St E) for lunch. This historic market has been around for over 200 years and offers a wide range of affordable food options. Grab a **peameal bacon sandwich** (a Toronto specialty) for about **$7-8 CAD** or sample artisanal cheeses, baked goods, and fresh produce.
- **Cost:** Free to enter, meals **$5-10 CAD**
- **How to get there:** Take the **King streetcar** to **Jarvis St**.

Afternoon: Royal Ontario Museum (ROM)

- Spend the afternoon at the **Royal Ontario Museum** (100 Queens Park), where you can explore everything from dinosaur fossils to ancient Egyptian artifacts. If you're visiting on the third Monday of the month, you can get free admission to the museum's permanent galleries from **5:30 PM to 8:30 PM**.
- **Cost:** Regular admission is **$23 CAD** for adults, free on select Mondays.
- **How to get there:** Take the **Line 1 subway** to **Museum Station**.

Day 4: A Day Trip to Niagara Falls

No visit to Toronto is complete without a day trip to **Niagara Falls**, one of the most iconic natural attractions in the world. You can visit the falls on a budget by using public transit and packing your own snacks for the day.

Morning: Travel to Niagara Falls

Take the **Go Transit** bus or train from **Union Station** to **Niagara Falls**. A round-trip ticket costs about **$30-35 CAD**, and the journey takes around 2 hours each way.

- **Cost:** Go Transit round-trip fare **$30-35 CAD**
- **How to get there:** Go Transit bus or train from **Union Station**.

Afternoon: Explore Niagara Falls

Once you arrive, you can walk along the **Niagara Parkway** to get stunning views of the falls for free. If you're feeling adventurous, you can take a ride on the **Niagara City Cruises** boat tour for **$28 CAD**, which takes you right up to the base of the falls. If you prefer to stay on dry land, there are plenty of free walking paths, gardens, and scenic viewpoints to explore.

- **Evening: Return to Toronto**
  - After spending the afternoon at the falls, catch the Go Transit bus or train back to Toronto in the early evening.

Day 5: Local Neighborhoods and Farewell

On your final day, take it easy by exploring some of Toronto's most interesting neighborhoods and grabbing a final budget-friendly meal before heading home.

Morning: Walk Through Queen Street West

Spend your morning strolling down **Queen Street West**, one of Toronto's trendiest neighborhoods. Known for its street art, independent boutiques, and cafes, Queen West is perfect for window shopping and enjoying the local vibe. Don't miss **Graffiti Alley**, a long stretch of colorful murals that's free to explore and perfect for photos.

- **Cost:** Free to explore
- **How to get there:** Take the **501 Queen streetcar** to **Bathurst St**.

Afternoon: Lunch in Chinatown

- End your trip with a budget-friendly meal in **Chinatown**. You'll find plenty of cheap and delicious eats, from dumplings to banh mi sandwiches. Try **Mother's Dumplings** (421 Spadina Ave), where you can get a plate of freshly made dumplings for about **$8-10 CAD**.
- **Cost:** Meals for **$8-12 CAD**
- **How to get there:** Take the **Spadina streetcar** to **Dundas St**.

Custom Itinerary Tips: Tailor Your Visit on a Budget

Every traveler has different interests, and creating a custom itinerary that suits your tastes can help you make the most of your visit while sticking to your budget. Here are some tips to help you build your own Toronto adventure, whether you're a foodie, nature lover, or history buff.

For Foodies

Toronto is a food lover's paradise, and you don't need to spend a fortune to eat well here. Stick to neighborhoods known for affordable eats and diverse cuisines.

Budget-Friendly Neighborhoods:

- **Chinatown** for dumplings and noodles.
- **Kensington Market** for international street food.
- **Little India** for affordable curries and samosas.

Top Picks:

- **Mother's Dumplings** for cheap dumplings in Chinatown ($8-10 CAD).
- **Seven Lives Tacos** in Kensington Market for huge, flavorful tacos ($7-10 CAD).
- **Lahore Tikka House** in Little India for filling, inexpensive South Asian meals ($10-15 CAD).

For Nature Lovers

Toronto and the surrounding areas offer beautiful green spaces and outdoor adventures, all at little to no cost.

Best Parks for Hiking and Relaxation:

- **High Park** for trails, ponds, and gardens (free).
- **Rouge National Urban Park** for longer hikes and camping (free).
- **Scarborough Bluffs** for stunning lake views (free).

Top Tips:

- Visit during off-peak times (early morning or weekdays) for fewer crowds.
- Pack your own food to enjoy a picnic and avoid spending money on snacks.

For History Buffs

Toronto is full of historic sites and museums that tell the story of the city's past.

Must-See Historical Sites:

- **Distillery District** for Victorian-era architecture (free to explore).
- **St. Lawrence Market** for a taste of Toronto's history and local food scene.
- **Fort York** for a deep dive into Toronto's military history (**$14 CAD** admission).

Budget Tips:

- Take advantage of free admission days at the **ROM** and **AGO** to explore their collections without paying full price.
- Use a **CityPass** if you plan to visit multiple paid attractions—it offers significant discounts on bundled tickets.

Entertainment and Fun

Free Festivals and Public Events: What to Look for in 2025

Toronto hosts numerous free festivals and public events every year, attracting locals and tourists alike. These events are a fantastic way to experience the city's diverse cultures, arts, and community spirit without spending a dime.

1. **Toronto Caribbean Carnival (Caribana)**

One of the biggest and most vibrant festivals in the city is the **Toronto Caribbean Carnival** (commonly known as **Caribana**), which celebrates Caribbean culture with music, dancing, and food. In 2025, this festival will take place over several weeks in July and August, with the highlight being the **Grand Parade**, which is free to attend and full of colorful costumes, lively music, and endless energy.

- **What to Expect:** The **Grand Parade** takes place along **Lakeshore Boulevard** and is the main event of Caribana, drawing hundreds of thousands of spectators. There are also free events leading up to the parade, such as outdoor concerts and community celebrations.
- **Budget Tip:** The parade itself is free to watch, but arrive early to secure a good spot along the route. Bring your own snacks and drinks to avoid buying from vendors.
- **Location:** Lakeshore Boulevard (Parade Route)

ENTERTAINMENT AND FUN

- **How to get there:** Take the **509 Harbourfront streetcar** to **Exhibition Place**.

2. **Luminato Festival**

The **Luminato Festival** (June 2025) is an annual arts and culture festival that features free public art installations, performances, and events across the city. It's a great opportunity to see innovative works by both local and international artists without spending money. The festival includes everything from visual arts to music and dance performances.

- **What to Expect:** In 2025, the Luminato Festival will showcase outdoor art installations in public spaces, free concerts in parks, and dance performances in venues across the city. Some events are ticketed, but many outdoor performances and art exhibits are free.
- **Budget Tip:** Check the festival's schedule online to find out which events are free, and plan to attend the outdoor performances and installations, which are often the most impressive and budget-friendly.
- **Location:** Various locations throughout Toronto
- **How to get there:** Check the festival's website for specific venues and directions.

3. **Toronto International Film Festival (TIFF) – Free Screenings and Events**

The **Toronto International Film Festival (TIFF)** is one of the world's most prestigious film festivals, and while many of the screenings are ticketed, there are also free events and outdoor screenings for budget travelers to enjoy. In 2025, TIFF will run from early to mid-September, and you can catch free outdoor screenings at **David Pecaut Square** during the festival.

- **What to Expect:** TIFF offers free screenings of classic films and family-friendly movies at **David Pecaut Square** during the festival. You can

also attend free talks and panel discussions with filmmakers and actors, which are open to the public.
- **Budget Tip:** Bring a blanket or folding chair to the outdoor screenings, and arrive early to grab a good spot. Check the TIFF website closer to the event for the full schedule of free events.
- **Location:** David Pecaut Square, 215 King St W, Toronto
- **How to get there:** Take the **King streetcar** to **Simcoe St** or walk from **St. Andrew Station**.

4. Scotiabank Nuit Blanche

Nuit Blanche is a free, all-night contemporary art festival held in early October that transforms Toronto's streets into a giant open-air gallery. The event features large-scale art installations, interactive exhibits, and performances spread across different neighborhoods.

- **What to Expect:** Hundreds of artists will display their works in public spaces throughout the city. You'll find everything from light shows to immersive sound installations, with many of the artworks encouraging public participation.
- **Budget Tip:** Wear comfortable shoes and plan to walk between different art installations. Some neighborhoods will have free shuttle buses to help you get around.
- **Location:** Various locations across Toronto
- **How to get there:** Use public transit, as many streets will be closed for the event.

5. Taste of the Danforth

In August 2025, the **Taste of the Danforth** festival will return to Toronto's **Greektown** neighborhood. This free event celebrates Greek culture with live music, dance performances, and, of course, plenty of food. While the food vendors charge for their dishes, many activities are free to enjoy, including live performances and cooking demonstrations.

- **What to Expect:** Live music, traditional Greek dancing, and plenty of food stalls lining **Danforth Avenue**. While food is sold at a cost, many vendors offer small plates for as low as **$5 CAD**, allowing you to sample several different dishes.
- **Budget Tip:** Enjoy the free entertainment, and look for food vendors offering affordable, small plates so you can sample a variety of dishes without overspending.
- **Location:** Danforth Avenue (between Broadview Ave and Pape Ave)
- **How to get there:** Take the **Line 2 subway** to **Chester Station** or **Pape Station**.

Budget-Friendly Cultural Experiences: Theater, Art, and Music

1. Free Outdoor Concerts at Harbourfront Centre

During the summer months, **Harbourfront Centre** (235 Queens Quay W, Toronto, ON M5J 2G8) hosts free outdoor concerts and cultural performances as part of its **Summer Music in the Garden** series. These concerts take place in the beautiful **Toronto Music Garden** along the waterfront and feature a wide range of musical genres, from classical to jazz.

- **What to Expect:** Free concerts in a peaceful garden setting. Bring a blanket or folding chair, and enjoy an evening of live music surrounded by nature.
- **Budget Tip:** The concerts are free, but food at Harbourfront can be expensive, so consider bringing your own snacks or picnic to enjoy during the performance.
- **Location:** Toronto Music Garden, 479 Queens Quay W, Toronto
- **How to get there:** Take the **509 Harbourfront streetcar** to **Queens**

Quay W.

2. Affordable Theater Productions at the Tarragon Theatre

If you're a fan of live theater but don't want to spend a lot, check out the **Tarragon Theatre** (30 Bridgman Ave, Toronto, ON M5R 1X3). This local theater offers affordable tickets to its productions, often showcasing original Canadian plays. The theater frequently has discounted tickets for students, seniors, and early-bird purchases, making it one of the most budget-friendly ways to experience live theater in Toronto.

- **What to Expect:** High-quality productions featuring Canadian playwrights and actors. Tarragon is known for its intimate setting and thought-provoking plays.
- **Budget Tip:** Look for **Pay-What-You-Can** performances, which are typically held on select Sundays. You can pay as little as **$10 CAD** to see a live theater show.
- **Location:** Tarragon Theatre, 30 Bridgman Ave, Toronto
- **How to get there:** Take the **Line 1 subway** to **Dupont Station**.

3. Free Art Exhibitions at The Power Plant

For contemporary art lovers, **The Power Plant** (231 Queens Quay W, Toronto, ON M5J 2G8) is a must-visit gallery that offers free admission to its exhibits. Located at Harbourfront Centre, The Power Plant showcases works from both Canadian and international artists, often featuring cutting-edge installations and multimedia exhibits.

- **What to Expect:** Free access to contemporary art exhibitions that change throughout the year. The gallery focuses on thought-provoking, sometimes experimental pieces, making it an exciting spot for art lovers.
- **Budget Tip:** Visit during opening receptions or special events to hear artists talk about their work—these events are often free to attend.

- **Location:** The Power Plant, 231 Queens Quay W, Toronto
- **How to get there:** Take the **509 Harbourfront streetcar** to **Queens Quay W**.

4. Live Jazz at The Rex Hotel Jazz & Blues Bar

The **Rex Hotel Jazz & Blues Bar** (194 Queen St W, Toronto, ON M5V 1Z1) is one of Toronto's most iconic live music venues. Known for its affordable cover charges, this venue features live jazz performances every night of the week, with many shows costing as little as **$10-15 CAD**. It's a great place to experience Toronto's jazz scene without overspending.

- **What to Expect:** A cozy, laid-back atmosphere with talented local and international jazz musicians performing live. The Rex is an intimate venue, so you'll be close to the action no matter where you sit.
- **Budget Tip:** Check out their early evening shows, which often have lower cover charges, or attend a weekday performance for the most affordable experience.
- **Location:** The Rex Hotel Jazz & Blues Bar, 194 Queen St W, Toronto
- **How to get there:** Take the **501 Queen streetcar** to **University Ave**.

5. AGO Free Wednesday Evenings

The **Art Gallery of Ontario (AGO)** (317 Dundas St W, Toronto, ON M5T 1G4) offers free admission to its permanent collection every Wednesday from **6:00 PM to 9:00 PM**. It's a fantastic opportunity to explore one of Canada's largest art museums without paying the regular **$25 CAD** admission fee. The AGO's collection includes works by Canadian artists, European masters, and contemporary pieces.

- **What to Expect:** Free access to the permanent galleries, which include Canadian landscapes, Indigenous art, and contemporary installations. You can easily spend a few hours wandering through the museum's many exhibits.

- **Budget Tip:** Arrive early, as free evenings can get busy. Plan your visit ahead of time to focus on the galleries you're most interested in seeing.
- **Location:** Art Gallery of Ontario, 317 Dundas St W, Toronto
- **How to get there:** Take the **505 Dundas streetcar** to **McCaul St.**

6. Shakespeare in High Park

Every summer, **Shakespeare in High Park** offers free outdoor performances of Shakespeare's plays in **High Park** (1873 Bloor St W). This long-standing Toronto tradition is a fantastic way to enjoy live theater in a relaxed, outdoor setting.

- **What to Expect:** Two different Shakespeare plays are performed on alternating nights throughout the summer. You can bring your own blanket or folding chair and enjoy a picnic while watching the performance. While admission is technically free, donations are encouraged.
- **Budget Tip:** Arrive early to grab a good spot, as seating is first-come, first-served. Pack your own snacks and drinks to enjoy during the show.
- **Location:** High Park Amphitheatre, 1873 Bloor St W, Toronto
- **How to get there:** Take the **Line 2 subway** to **High Park Station**.

Sports on a Budget: Toronto Blue Jays and Raptors Game Day Tips

Toronto Blue Jays Game Day Tips

The Toronto Blue Jays play at **Rogers Centre** (1 Blue Jays Way, Toronto, ON M5V 1J1), right in the heart of downtown Toronto. Whether you're a baseball fan or just looking for a fun day out, attending a game is an exciting experience.

ENTERTAINMENT AND FUN

Budget Tip 1: Look for Cheap Tickets on Value Days

The Blue Jays often have **Value Days**, where you can find tickets starting as low as **$15 CAD** for certain games, particularly during weekday games or when they're playing less popular teams. These value days are usually midweek games (Tuesday or Wednesday), and ticket prices are much cheaper than weekend games or when the team is playing rivals.

Budget Tip 2: Upper Deck Seating

The most affordable seats are in the upper deck (Level 500), where you can often find tickets for around **$20 CAD**. While these seats are further from the action, you still get a great view of the game, and the atmosphere is just as lively. You can also walk around the stadium to check out different views and enjoy the ballpark experience from various angles.

Budget Tip 3: Score Last-Minute Deals

- If you're flexible, you can sometimes find last-minute deals on websites like **StubHub** or **SeatGeek**, where fans resell their tickets. You can often score cheaper tickets closer to game day, especially for games that aren't sold out.

Budget Tip 4: Bring Your Own Food

Food and drinks inside Rogers Centre can be pricey, but the good news is that the stadium allows you to bring your own food. Pack a sandwich, snacks, and a bottle of water to save on concession stand prices, where items can cost upwards of **$10-15 CAD** for basic snacks.

- **Location:** Rogers Centre, 1 Blue Jays Way, Toronto, ON M5V 1J1
- **Cost:** Tickets start at **$15-20 CAD** on Value Days
- **How to get there:** Take the **Line 1 subway** to **Union Station**, and the stadium is a short walk away.

Toronto Raptors Game Day Tips

The **Toronto Raptors** play their home games at **Scotiabank Arena** (40 Bay St, Toronto, ON M5J 2X2). Raptors games are incredibly popular, especially since their 2019 NBA Championship win, but there are ways to attend a game without blowing your budget.

Budget Tip 1: Weekday Games Are Cheaper

Like the Blue Jays, Raptors tickets tend to be cheaper on weekdays, especially earlier in the season or when they're playing less popular teams. Look for games on Monday, Tuesday, or Wednesday nights for the best deals, with tickets starting around **$30-40 CAD** in the upper sections.

Budget Tip 2: Fan-to-Fan Ticket Exchanges

Websites like **Ticketmaster's Verified Resale** or **StubHub** often have fans reselling their tickets, sometimes at lower prices than official outlets. Keep an eye on these sites for last-minute discounts, especially if you're not picky about where you sit.

Budget Tip 3: Raptors 905

If you want to experience a professional basketball game but don't want to pay Raptors prices, consider attending a **Raptors 905** game. Raptors 905 is the Raptors' G-League affiliate, and they play at the **Paramount Fine Foods Centre** in Mississauga, a short drive or public transit ride from Toronto. Tickets for Raptors 905 games are much more affordable, starting around **$20 CAD**, and it's a fun way to see up-and-coming talent.

- **Location:** Scotiabank Arena, 40 Bay St, Toronto, ON M5J 2X2
- **Cost:** Raptors tickets start at **$30-40 CAD** for weekday games
- **How to get there:** Take the **Line 1 subway** to **Union Station**, and the arena is connected via the **PATH** system.

ENTERTAINMENT AND FUN

Cheap Movie Nights and Affordable Cinemas

If you're a movie lover, Toronto has plenty of affordable options for catching the latest films or enjoying classic flicks on a budget. Whether you prefer traditional cinemas or free outdoor screenings, here are some tips for enjoying movies without spending too much.

Discounted Movie Nights

Several cinemas across Toronto offer discounted movie nights, usually on **Tuesdays**, making it the best day of the week to catch a film if you're on a budget.

Cineplex Cinemas

Cineplex, the largest cinema chain in Canada, offers **Discount Tuesdays** at all of its locations, where tickets are typically priced around **$9-10 CAD** compared to the usual **$13-16 CAD**. This deal is available for both regular and VIP seating, so you can enjoy a luxury experience for a lower price. Make sure to check their **Scene+ Rewards Program**, where you can earn points for free tickets and snacks.

- **Locations:** Cineplex cinemas are found all over Toronto, with major locations at **Yonge-Dundas** (10 Dundas St E), **Scotiabank Theatre** (259 Richmond St W), and **Cineplex VIP at The Shops at Don Mills** (1090 Don Mills Rd).
- **Cost:** Tickets around **$9-10 CAD** on Tuesdays
- **How to get there:** Easily accessible by public transit; check individual locations for details.

Imagine Cinemas

For an even more affordable option, **Imagine Cinemas** (80 Front St E, Toronto, ON M5E 1T4) offers discounted tickets throughout the week, with prices starting around **$10 CAD** for regular showings. The cinema is located right near **St. Lawrence Market**, making it a great option if you want to catch a film after exploring the market during the day.

- **Location:** Imagine Cinemas Market Square, 80 Front St E, Toronto, ON M5E 1T4
- **Cost:** Tickets around **$10 CAD**
- **How to get there:** Take the **King streetcar** to **Jarvis St.**

Free Outdoor Movie Screenings

During the summer months, Toronto hosts several free outdoor movie nights in parks and public spaces. These events are perfect for enjoying a movie under the stars, and all you need is a blanket or lawn chair to join in.

Sail-In Cinema (Sugar Beach)

One of the most unique free movie experiences in Toronto is **Sail-In Cinema** at **Sugar Beach** (25 Dockside Dr, Toronto, ON M5A 0B5). The event features a giant floating screen, and attendees can watch the movie either from the shore or from boats anchored in the water. Held in August, Sail-In Cinema offers family-friendly films and a lively atmosphere by the lake.

- **Cost:** Free
- **How to get there:** Take the **6 Bay bus** to **Queens Quay East**.

Christie Pits Film Festival

Another popular outdoor movie series is the **Christie Pits Film Festival**, which runs from June to August at **Christie Pits Park** (750 Bloor St W, Toronto, ON M6G 3K4). The festival features a mix of classic films and recent releases, and it's completely free, although donations are encouraged. Bring your own blanket, snacks, and friends for a laid-back movie night in the park.

- **Cost:** Free (donations welcome)
- **How to get there:** Take the **Line 2 subway** to **Christie Station**.

Under the Stars (Regent Park)

Under the Stars is another free outdoor movie series hosted at **Regent Park** (620 Dundas St E, Toronto, ON M5A 3S9) throughout the summer. It's a family-friendly event that screens a diverse range of films, from recent hits to cult classics, with the added bonus of live performances and food vendors before the movie starts.

- **Cost:** Free
- **How to get there:** Take the **505 Dundas streetcar** to **Dundas St East and Parliament St**.

General Tips for Budget Entertainment in Toronto

- **Check for Promotions:** Always check for deals on websites like **Groupon** or **LivingSocial**, where you can often find discounted tickets for events, movie theaters, or sporting events.
- **Sign Up for Loyalty Programs:** Whether it's **Scene+ Rewards** at Cineplex or email alerts from **Ticketmaster**, signing up for loyalty programs and alerts can help you score discounts or early access to promotions.
- **Explore Free Events:** Toronto is home to many free events throughout the year, from concerts and festivals to movie screenings. Websites like **BlogTO** and **Toronto.com** list upcoming events, many of which are free or low-cost.

Outdoor Adventures: Kayaking, Biking, and More on a Budget

1. Kayaking Along Toronto's Waterfront

Kayaking is one of the best ways to experience Toronto's beautiful waterfront, offering a unique perspective of the city skyline and the islands. Whether you're a seasoned kayaker or a beginner, there are plenty of places to rent kayaks without spending too much.

Where to Go:
The most popular place to kayak in Toronto is around the **Toronto Islands**, a short ferry ride from the city. The calm waters between the islands and the mainland make it perfect for beginners and seasoned paddlers alike. You can also kayak along **Harbourfront** and the **Humber River** for a more urban adventure.

Affordable Rentals:
Harbourfront Canoe & Kayak Centre (283A Queen's Quay West, Toronto, ON M5V 1A2) offers affordable kayak rentals. Single kayaks cost around **$25 CAD per hour**, while tandem kayaks are **$40 CAD per hour**. This is one of the most accessible rental spots, located right on the waterfront.

Toronto Island SUP (9 Queens Quay West, Toronto, ON M5J 2H3) also offers kayak rentals for about **$30 CAD per hour**, with discounted rates for half-day rentals if you want to explore the islands at a more leisurely pace.

Budget Tip:
If you plan to spend more time on the water, consider renting for half a day or a full day. Many rental spots offer discounts for longer rentals. Additionally, pack your own snacks and water to avoid buying expensive refreshments on the islands.

Harbourfront Canoe & Kayak Centre:

Address: 283A Queen's Quay West, Toronto, ON M5V 1A2
Cost: Single kayak **$25 CAD per hour**, tandem kayak **$40 CAD per hour**
How to get there: Take the **509 Harbourfront streetcar** to Queens Quay W.

2. Biking Along Toronto's Waterfront

Biking is one of the most budget-friendly and eco-friendly ways to explore Toronto. The city is becoming more bike-friendly, and there are plenty of scenic trails along the waterfront, through parks, and even around the Toronto Islands.

Where to Ride:

Martin Goodman Trail: This multi-use trail stretches for over 56 kilometers along the Toronto waterfront. It's perfect for a leisurely bike ride and offers beautiful views of Lake Ontario. You can start anywhere along the waterfront, but a great place to begin is near **Harbourfront Centre** (235 Queens Quay W).

Toronto Islands: If you take the ferry to the **Toronto Islands**, you can bike around the islands on car-free roads. It's a peaceful way to explore the natural beauty of the islands while getting some exercise. There are plenty of picnic spots and beaches where you can stop for a break.

Affordable Bike Rentals:

Bike Share Toronto is a convenient and affordable option for short bike rides around the city. You can rent bikes at any of the Bike Share stations, which are located all over Toronto. A single ride costs **$3.25 CAD for 30 minutes**, and a day pass (which includes unlimited 30-minute rides for 24 hours) costs **$7 CAD**. If you're planning to bike for a few days, you can get a monthly membership for **$25 CAD**.

If you want to rent a bike for a longer period, **Wheel Excitement** (249 Queens Quay W, Toronto, ON M5J 2N5) rents out bikes for about **$12 CAD per hour** or **$45 CAD for a full day**.

Budget Tip:

Use **Bike Share Toronto** for short trips or to explore multiple parts of the city in one day. You can pick up and drop off bikes at different locations, making it easier to cover more ground. If you're biking on the islands, bring your own bike on the ferry for a small fee (about **$8.70 CAD** round trip for the ferry).

Bike Share Toronto:
   Cost: Single ride **$3.25 CAD for 30 minutes**, day pass **$7 CAD**
   Website: Bike Share Toronto
   How to get there: Bike Share stations are located throughout the city.

3. **Hiking and Nature Trails**

Toronto is surrounded by beautiful parks and nature trails that are perfect for hiking and walking. Many of these spots are free to enter, making them ideal for budget travelers who want to enjoy the outdoors without spending money.

High Park

High Park (1873 Bloor St W, Toronto, ON M6R 2Z3) is one of the largest parks in Toronto and offers a variety of hiking trails, from easy walks to more challenging routes. You can explore the gardens, walk around **Grenadier Pond**, or visit the small zoo that's free to enter. The park is especially beautiful in the spring when the cherry blossoms are in bloom, and in the fall when the leaves change color.

- **Cost:** Free
- **How to get there:** Take the **Line 2 subway** to **High Park Station**.

Rouge National Urban Park

If you're looking for a more challenging hike, head to **Rouge National Urban Park** (1749 Meadowvale Rd, Toronto, ON M1B 5W8), which is just outside the city. This park offers a variety of trails through forests, wetlands, and meadows. The **Vista Trail** is a popular route that offers beautiful views of the Rouge River and surrounding landscapes.

- **Cost:** Free
- **How to get there:** Take the **85 Sheppard East bus** from **Don Mills Station** to **Meadowvale Rd**.

Don Valley Trails

The **Don Valley Trails** are a network of scenic hiking and biking paths that run through the heart of Toronto along the Don River. The **Lower Don Trail** is a popular route that connects to several parks, including **Riverdale Park** and **Evergreen Brick Works**. It's a peaceful escape from the busy city, and it's completely free to explore.

- **Cost:** Free
- **How to get there:** Take the **Line 2 subway** to **Broadview Station** and walk into the valley.

4. Paddleboarding on Lake Ontario

If you're looking for a fun and affordable water activity, try **stand-up paddleboarding (SUP)**. Paddleboarding is a great way to enjoy Lake Ontario and get a little exercise at the same time.

Where to Go:

The **Toronto Islands** and **Harbourfront** are two of the best spots for paddleboarding. The waters around the islands are calm, making it easier for beginners to learn, while the Harbourfront offers amazing views of the city skyline.

Affordable Rentals:

Toronto Island SUP (9 Queens Quay West, Toronto, ON M5J 2G8) offers paddleboard rentals for around **$30 CAD per hour**. They also provide lessons if you're new to the sport.

The Beaches Paddleboarding is another great option, with rentals starting at **$25 CAD per hour**. It's located in the **Beaches** neighborhood, and you can paddle out onto the calm waters of **Woodbine Beach**.

Budget Tip:
Book a rental during off-peak hours (early morning or late afternoon) to avoid crowds and save money. If you're confident in your skills, renting for a half-day or full-day can give you more time on the water at a lower rate.

Toronto Island SUP:
Cost: Paddleboard rental **$30 CAD per hour**
Location: 9 Queens Quay West, Toronto, ON M5J 2G8
How to get there: Take the **Toronto Island Ferry** to the islands or the **509 Harbourfront streetcar** to Queens Quay W.

5. **Picnicking in Toronto's Parks**
Sometimes the best outdoor adventures are the simplest ones. Toronto has many beautiful parks where you can relax and enjoy a picnic without spending much. Pack your own food from a local grocery store or farmer's market, and find a quiet spot to unwind.

Best Picnic Spots:

- **Trinity Bellwoods Park** (790 Queen St W, Toronto, ON M6J 1G3): A trendy park in the west end, popular with locals for picnics and outdoor gatherings.
- **Riverdale Park** (550 Broadview Ave, Toronto, ON M4K 2N6): Offers beautiful views of the Toronto skyline and is a great spot to relax with friends.

- **Woodbine Beach** (1675 Lake Shore Blvd E, Toronto, ON M4L 3W6): Perfect for a beach picnic, with plenty of space to spread out on the sand.

Budget Tip:

Buy picnic supplies from **Kensington Market** or **St. Lawrence Market**, where you can find affordable, fresh food. Bring your own drinks, as prices at nearby kiosks or cafes tend to be higher.

Woodbine Beach:
  Location: 1675 Lake Shore Blvd E, Toronto, ON M4L 3W6
  Cost: Free to access
  How to get there: Take the **501 Queen streetcar** to **Woodbine Ave.**

Tips for Saving on Outdoor Gear Rentals

Outdoor activities don't have to be expensive, especially if you know where to find affordable gear rentals. Here are some tips to help you save on renting bikes, kayaks, paddleboards, and other equipment:

- **Book in Advance:** Many rental companies offer discounts if you book online in advance. Check their websites for deals or promotions.
- **Choose Off-Peak Times:** Rates are often lower during weekdays or early in the morning. If you can, avoid renting during weekends or holidays when demand is higher.
- **Share Rentals:** If you're with friends, consider sharing a tandem kayak or renting a paddleboard for two people. This can cut costs and make the experience more affordable.
- **Bring Your Own Gear:** If you're planning to bike, hike, or paddle frequently, it might be worth investing in your own equipment. For example, bringing your own bike on the ferry to the Toronto Islands only costs **$8.70 CAD** for a round trip, compared to renting a bike for

the day.

Toronto for Families on a Budget

Family-Friendly Accommodations: Hotels and Rentals with Budget Options

1. **The Novotel Toronto Centre**

Located near **St. Lawrence Market** and **Harbourfront**, **Novotel Toronto Centre** (45 The Esplanade, Toronto, ON M5E 1W2) is a great choice for families looking for budget-friendly accommodations in downtown Toronto. The hotel offers spacious rooms, many of which include two double beds, perfect for families. Some rooms also come with mini-fridges and microwaves, making it easier to store snacks and prepare quick meals.

Family-Friendly Amenities:

- Family rooms with two double beds
- Indoor pool
- Free Wi-Fi
- On-site restaurant with a kids' menu
- **Cost:** Rates typically start around **$150-180 CAD per night** depending on the season.
- **Neighborhood: St. Lawrence Market** is within walking distance, and you'll also be close to popular attractions like **Ripley's Aquarium** and **Harbourfront**.
- **Address:** Novotel Toronto Centre, 45 The Esplanade, Toronto, ON

M5E 1W2
- **How to get there:** Take the **Line 1 subway** to **Union Station**, and the hotel is a short walk from there.
- **Cost: $150-180 CAD per night**

2. **Town Inn Suites**

For families who prefer the convenience of a kitchenette, **Town Inn Suites** (620 Church St, Toronto, ON M4Y 2G2) offers spacious apartment-style accommodations. Each suite comes with a full kitchen, living area, and separate bedroom, which is perfect for families who want a bit more space and the option to cook their own meals. The hotel is located near **Bloor Street**, giving you access to shopping, dining, and parks.

Family-Friendly Amenities:

- Full kitchen in every suite
- Indoor pool
- Free Wi-Fi
- On-site laundry facilities
- **Cost:** Rates start at **$160-200 CAD per night**, which is great value considering the extra space and kitchen amenities.
- **Neighborhood:** Located in **Yorkville**, this area is safe and family-friendly, with plenty of parks nearby, including **Queen's Park** and **Ramsden Park**.
- **Address:** Town Inn Suites, 620 Church St, Toronto, ON M4Y 2G2
- **How to get there:** Take the **Line 1 subway** to **Bloor-Yonge Station** and walk a few blocks to the hotel.
- **Cost: $160-200 CAD per night**

3. **The Rex Hotel**

For a more budget-friendly option in the downtown area, **The Rex Hotel** (194 Queen St W, Toronto, ON M5V 1Z1) offers basic but comfortable accommodations. While it's known as a jazz bar, it also has a small selection of affordable family rooms. The location on **Queen Street West** is perfect for exploring **Kensington Market**, **Graffiti Alley**, and the **Toronto Eaton Centre**.

Family-Friendly Amenities:

- Rooms with two double beds
- Free Wi-Fi
- On-site restaurant and live music (the music is usually family-friendly earlier in the evening)
- **Cost:** Rooms start at **$130-150 CAD per night**, making it one of the more affordable options in the heart of downtown Toronto.
- **Neighborhood:** Close to popular attractions like **Nathan Phillips Square** and **Art Gallery of Ontario (AGO)**.
- **Address:** The Rex Hotel, 194 Queen St W, Toronto, ON M5V 1Z1
- **How to get there:** Take the **501 Queen streetcar** to **University Ave.**
- **Cost: $130-150 CAD per night**

4. **Airbnb and Vacation Rentals**

For families who need more space or want to stay in a quieter neighborhood, Airbnb and vacation rentals are a great option. You can find affordable family-friendly rentals with multiple bedrooms, kitchenettes, and easy access to public transport. Neighborhoods like **The Beaches**, **Leslieville**, and **Danforth** offer great value, with proximity to parks, family-friendly cafes, and local attractions.

Neighborhoods for Families:

- **The Beaches**: This neighborhood offers easy access to **Woodbine Beach** and **Kew Gardens**, along with a variety of playgrounds and kid-friendly restaurants.

- **Leslieville**: Known for its family-friendly vibe, Leslieville is close to several parks and playgrounds, and it's only a short streetcar ride to downtown Toronto.
- **Danforth**: A quieter area with a strong Greek community, Danforth offers great food, parks, and easy access to **Toronto Zoo**.
- **Cost:** Rentals typically range from **$100-200 CAD per night**, depending on the size of the home and its location.

Neighborhoods Offering the Best Value for Families

- **East End (The Beaches, Leslieville, Danforth):** These neighborhoods offer access to parks, beaches, and affordable family dining. They're also close enough to downtown attractions without the higher hotel prices.
- **Yorkville:** If you want to stay closer to downtown, Yorkville offers family-friendly accommodations with access to parks, shopping, and museums.
- **Midtown:** Areas like **Davisville Village** and **Yonge-Eglinton** offer great value with proximity to parks, playgrounds, and family-friendly restaurants.

Free and Cheap Activities for Kids

1. High Park

High Park (1873 Bloor St W, Toronto, ON M6R 2Z3) is a perfect spot for families looking to spend time outdoors. It's one of the largest parks in Toronto and offers a variety of free activities, including hiking trails, picnic areas, and a small zoo.

Family-Friendly Attractions:

- **High Park Zoo**: Free to visit, the zoo features animals like bison, llamas,

and peacocks.
- **Jamie Bell Adventure Playground**: This huge wooden playground is a hit with kids of all ages, offering plenty of climbing structures and slides.
- **Cost:** Free
- **Location:** 1873 Bloor St W, Toronto, ON M6R 2Z3
- **How to get there:** Take the **Line 2 subway** to **High Park Station**.

2. Riverdale Farm

Riverdale Farm (201 Winchester St, Toronto, ON M4X 1B8) is a free, family-friendly attraction located in the heart of downtown. It's a working farm that's home to cows, goats, chickens, and pigs, and it's a great way for kids to experience farm life without leaving the city.

Attractions:

- Animal barns and paddocks where kids can see farm animals up close.
- Walking trails through a scenic park.
- **Cost:** Free
- **Location:** 201 Winchester St, Toronto, ON M4X 1B8
- **How to get there:** Take the **506 Carlton streetcar** to **Parliament St**.

3. Ontario Science Centre

The **Ontario Science Centre** (770 Don Mills Rd, North York, ON M3C 1T3) is one of the most interactive and kid-friendly museums in the city. It features hands-on exhibits that teach kids about science, technology, and nature. While general admission costs **$22 CAD** for adults and **$13 CAD** for kids, it's well worth the price for a full day of fun and learning.

Family-Friendly Exhibits:

- **KidSpark**: A section designed specifically for kids 8 and under, with interactive exhibits on building, water play, and more.
- **The Space Hall**: Kids can explore the wonders of space, including a planetarium and astronaut displays.
- **Cost:** Adults **$22 CAD**, children **$13 CAD**
- **Location:** 770 Don Mills Rd, North York, ON M3C 1T3
- **How to get there:** Take the **25 Don Mills bus** from **Pape Station**.

4. Toronto Island Park

A visit to **Toronto Island Park** is a great way to spend a day with kids without spending much. The ferry ride itself is a fun experience for kids, and once you arrive, there are plenty of free or low-cost activities to enjoy.

Family-Friendly Activities:

- **Centreville Amusement Park**: While entry is free, individual rides cost around **$3-6 CAD**.
- **Franklin Children's Garden**: A free, interactive garden where kids can explore nature and climb play structures.
- **Cost:** Ferry ride is **$8.70 CAD** for adults, **$4.10 CAD** for children
- **Location:** Take the ferry from **Jack Layton Ferry Terminal** (9 Queens Quay W, Toronto, ON M5J 2H3)
- **How to get there:** Take the **509 Harbourfront streetcar** to **Queens Quay W**.

5. Evergreen Brick Works

Located in the **Don Valley, Evergreen Brick Works** (550 Bayview Ave, Toronto, ON M4W 3X8) is an outdoor park and community center that's perfect for families. There are hiking trails, ponds, and even a weekly farmer's market where you can pick up local food.

Activities for Kids:

- **Children's Garden**: An interactive play area where kids can learn about nature, dig in the soil, and get their hands dirty.
- **Bike Rentals**: Rent a bike and ride the trails around the park, or bring your own.
- **Cost:** Free to enter; bike rentals cost about **$10-15 CAD per hour**
- **Location:** 550 Bayview Ave, Toronto, ON M4W 3X8
- **How to get there:** Take the **28 Bayview South bus** from **Davisville Station.**

6. AGO's Family Sundays

The **Art Gallery of Ontario (AGO)** (317 Dundas St W, Toronto, ON M5T 1G4) offers free entry for children under 25, and they host **Family Sundays**, which include special art activities and workshops designed for kids. This is a great way to introduce your children to art without spending much.

Family-Friendly Attractions:

- Free entry for kids and hands-on art-making activities.
- Interactive exhibits and galleries that are designed with families in mind.
- **Cost:** Free for children under 25; adult admission **$25 CAD**
- **Location:** 317 Dundas St W, Toronto, ON M5T 1G4
- **How to get there:** Take the **505 Dundas streetcar** to **McCaul St.**

7. ROM's Friday Night Free Admission

The **Royal Ontario Museum (ROM)** (100 Queens Park, Toronto, ON M5S 2C6) is one of the best family-friendly attractions in the city, and on the third Monday of every month, admission to the museum's permanent galleries is free from **5:30 PM to 8:30 PM**. This makes it a great budget-friendly option for families who want to explore exhibits on dinosaurs, ancient Egypt, and more.

Cost: Free on the third Monday of the month; regular admission **$23 CAD** for adults, **$18 CAD** for children

Location: 100 Queens Park, Toronto, ON M5S 2C6

How to get there: Take the **Line 1 subway** to **Museum Station**.

Top Parks and Playgrounds for Families

1. High Park

High Park (1873 Bloor St W, Toronto, ON M6R 2Z3) is one of Toronto's largest and most family-friendly parks. It offers an abundance of free activities for children, including multiple playgrounds, splash pads, and even a small zoo that's free to visit. Families can easily spend an entire day here without spending a dime.

- **Playgrounds and Splash Pads:** High Park's **Jamie Bell Adventure Playground** is a hit with kids, featuring large wooden structures, slides, swings, and climbing areas. During the summer, the **wading pool** and **splash pad** near the playground are open, offering a fun way for kids to cool off.
- **Picnic Areas:** High Park has plenty of shaded picnic spots, including large grassy areas where you can spread out a blanket. There are also picnic tables scattered throughout the park, many near the playgrounds and splash pads.
- **Other Family-Friendly Amenities:** The **High Park Zoo** is a small, free zoo featuring animals like bison, llamas, and peacocks. The park also has several walking trails, perfect for families who enjoy a casual stroll through nature.
- **Location:** High Park 1873 Bloor St W, Toronto, ON M6R 2Z3
- **How to get there:** Take the **Line 2 subway** to **High Park Station**.
- **Cost:** Free

2. Riverdale Park East

Riverdale Park East (550 Broadview Ave, Toronto, ON M4K 2N6) is another great spot for families. With stunning views of the Toronto skyline and plenty of space to run and play, it's a perfect choice for a day out with the kids.

- **Playground and Splash Pad:** The park's **playground** is well-equipped with slides, swings, and climbing structures, suitable for children of all ages. During the summer, the **splash pad** is open, offering a free, fun activity for kids to enjoy.
- **Picnic Areas:** Riverdale Park East has several picnic tables and benches, but the real draw is the large grassy hill, which is perfect for spreading out a picnic blanket. The hill also offers incredible views of the city, making it a relaxing spot for families.
- **Other Family-Friendly Amenities:** In the winter, the park's hill becomes a popular spot for tobogganing, and in the summer, there are baseball fields and tennis courts that can be used for free on a first-come, first-served basis.
- **Location:** Riverdale Park East 550 Broadview Ave, Toronto, ON M4K 2N6
- **How to get there:** Take the **504 King streetcar** to **Broadview Station** and walk south.
- **Cost:** Free

3. Kew Gardens and Woodbine Beach

Located in the **Beaches** neighborhood, **Kew Gardens** (2075 Queen St E, Toronto, ON M4E 2N9) and **Woodbine Beach** offer a perfect combination of playgrounds, picnic areas, and waterfront fun. This is a great spot for families who want to spend a day outdoors near the lake.

- **Playground and Splash Pad:** Kew Gardens has a large playground with swings, slides, and climbing equipment. Just a short walk away,

the **Woodbine Beach splash pad** is a favorite for kids in the summer, offering a cool break after playing on the sand.
- **Picnic Areas:** There are plenty of picnic tables in **Kew Gardens**, as well as grassy areas where you can set up your own picnic. Woodbine Beach also has BBQ areas, making it easy to have a family cookout by the water.
- **Other Family-Friendly Amenities:** Woodbine Beach offers soft sand, shallow waters, and lifeguards during the summer months, making it a safe and fun beach for children. There are also walking paths and bike trails along the boardwalk.
- **Location:** Kew Gardens 2075 Queen St E, Toronto, ON M4E 2N9
- **How to get there:** Take the **501 Queen streetcar** to **Kew Gardens**.
- **Cost:** Free

4. **Trinity Bellwoods Park**

Trinity Bellwoods Park (790 Queen St W, Toronto, ON M6J 1G3) is a popular urban park located in the west end of the city. It's known for its wide open spaces, shaded areas, and family-friendly activities.

- **Playground and Splash Pad:** The park's playground is well-maintained and includes swings, slides, and climbing structures. There's also a **splash pad** nearby, perfect for cooling down on hot summer days.
- **Picnic Areas:** Trinity Bellwoods Park has plenty of open spaces and picnic tables, making it a popular spot for family picnics. There's a mix of sunny and shaded areas, so you can find a comfortable spot no matter the weather.
- **Other Family-Friendly Amenities:** The park is home to several large grassy fields where kids can run around or play sports. The nearby **Farmers' Market** (held on Tuesdays during the warmer months) is a great place to grab fresh, local snacks for your picnic.
- **Location:**Trinity Bellwoods Park790 Queen St W, Toronto, ON M6J 1G3

- **How to get there:** Take the **501 Queen streetcar** to **Queen St W and Strachan Ave**.
- **Cost:** Free

5. Corktown Common

Corktown Common (155 Bayview Ave, Toronto, ON M5A 1E1) is a modern, well-designed park that's perfect for families with young children. It offers a combination of playgrounds, splash pads, and picnic areas, making it a great spot for an all-day outing.

- **Playground and Splash Pad:** The playground at Corktown Common is new and includes state-of-the-art equipment, such as a water play area, climbing structures, and sandboxes. The **splash pad** is a big hit with kids during the summer.
- **Picnic Areas:** There are shaded picnic tables scattered throughout the park, as well as grassy areas for laying out a blanket. The park also has BBQ areas that are perfect for a family cookout.
- **Other Family-Friendly Amenities:** The park is designed to connect families with nature, featuring wetlands, gardens, and walking trails. There are also public washrooms and changing facilities, making it very family-friendly.
- **Location:** Corktown Common 155 Bayview Ave, Toronto, ON M5A 1E1
- **How to get there:** Take the **501 Queen streetcar** to **Bayview Ave**.
- **Cost:** Free

Budget Dining Options for Families

1. The Old Spaghetti Factory

A classic family-friendly dining spot in Toronto, **The Old Spaghetti Factory** (54 The Esplanade, Toronto, ON M5E 1A6) is known for its large portions and affordable prices. The restaurant has a fun, eclectic interior, making it a hit with kids, and it offers a variety of pasta dishes, salads, and more—all at budget-friendly prices.

- **Why it's great for families:** Kids will love the whimsical decor, and the menu offers generous portions at reasonable prices. A typical meal includes bread, soup or salad, the main course, and ice cream for dessert, all for around **$12-18 CAD** per person.
- **Kids' Menu:** The kids' menu features smaller portions of spaghetti, mac and cheese, and other kid-friendly options for around **$8-10 CAD**.
- **Location:** The Old Spaghetti Factory 54 The Esplanade, Toronto, ON M5E 1A6
- **How to get there:** Take the **504 King streetcar** to **Church St.**
- **Cost:** Meals range from **$12-18 CAD**, kids' menu **$8-10 CAD**

2. Fran's Restaurant

Fran's Restaurant (20 College St, Toronto, ON M5G 1K2) is a Toronto institution, known for its diner-style food and family-friendly atmosphere. It's a great place to take the kids for a casual meal, and the prices are affordable enough to feed the whole family without stress.

- **Why it's great for families:** The large menu includes something for everyone, from all-day breakfast to burgers and milkshakes. Portions are generous, and most meals cost between **$10-15 CAD**, making it easy to stick to a budget.
- **Kids' Menu:** Fran's offers kid-sized portions of favorites like pancakes, chicken fingers, and grilled cheese, with prices starting at **$6-8 CAD**.

- **Location:** Fran's Restaurant 20 College St, Toronto, ON M5G 1K2
- **How to get there:** Take the **Line 1 subway** to **College Station.**
- **Cost:** Meals range from **$10-15 CAD**, kids' menu **$6-8 CAD**

3. **St. Lawrence Market Food Court**

If you're looking for a quick, affordable bite that still satisfies everyone's tastes, head to the **St. Lawrence Market** (93 Front St E, Toronto, ON M5E 1C3). The market has a variety of food stalls offering budget-friendly meals, from sandwiches to international cuisines.

- **Why it's great for families:** There's plenty of seating, and the wide range of food options means everyone in the family can find something they like. You can grab sandwiches, burgers, or fresh salads for around **$5-10 CAD.**
- **Kids' Favorites:** The market has many kid-friendly options, including pizza, grilled cheese, and freshly made pastries.
- **Location:** St. Lawrence Market 93 Front St E, Toronto, ON M5E 1C3
- **How to get there:** Take the **King streetcar** to **Jarvis St.**
- **Cost:** Meals range from **$5-10 CAD**

4. **Jack Astor's Bar & Grill**

With several locations across Toronto, **Jack Astor's Bar & Grill** is a popular choice for families looking for a casual, budget-friendly meal. The restaurant offers a fun atmosphere with plenty of kid-friendly options.

- **Why it's great for families:** The portions are large, and the menu includes a wide variety of dishes, from burgers to pasta. Kids will love the interactive children's menu, which includes activities and games. Meals for adults typically cost between **$15-20 CAD**, while the kids' menu offers meals for **$7-10 CAD.**
- **Kids' Menu:** The kids' menu features favorites like chicken fingers,

mini burgers, and mac and cheese, all served with a drink and dessert.
- **Location:** Various locations throughout Toronto
- **Cost:** Adult meals **$15-20 CAD**, kids' menu **$7-10 CAD**
- **How to get there:** Locations vary; check their website for the nearest restaurant.

5. **Freshii**

For a healthier, budget-friendly option, **Freshii** (various locations across Toronto) offers a range of salads, wraps, bowls, and smoothies that are perfect for families on the go. Freshii focuses on fresh, healthy ingredients, and the portions are generous enough to share.

- **Why it's great for families:** Freshii's meals are healthy and customizable, making it easy to accommodate picky eaters. Most meals cost between **$10-15 CAD**, and you can share large bowls or wraps to keep costs down.
- **Kids' Options:** While there's no specific kids' menu, you can order smaller portions or build-your-own bowls with kid-friendly ingredients like rice, chicken, and veggies.
- **Location:** Various locations throughout Toronto
- **Cost:** Meals range from **$10-15 CAD**
- **How to get there:** Locations vary; check their website for the nearest restaurant.

Tips for Traveling with Kids on a Budget

1. **Transportation: Getting Around Affordably**

Getting around Toronto with kids can be simple and cost-effective, thanks to the city's public transportation system. With a little planning, you can explore Toronto's attractions without paying too much for transportation.

Use the TTC (Toronto Transit Commission)

- The TTC operates buses, streetcars, and subways throughout the city, and it's one of the most affordable ways to get around. If you're traveling as a family, children under **12 years old ride for free**, while adults and teens pay **$3.35 CAD** per trip. You can also purchase a **Day Pass** for **$13.50 CAD**, which covers unlimited rides for one adult and up to five children (under 12) or two adults and up to four children. This is perfect for families who plan to visit multiple attractions in a day.

Budget Tip:

- Use the **TTC Day Pass** on weekends and holidays to make the most of unlimited rides with your family. This allows you to visit different parts of the city without worrying about additional transit costs.

Walk Whenever Possible

- Toronto is a walkable city, especially downtown, where many major attractions are close to each other. Walking can save you money on transportation while giving you and your kids the chance to enjoy the sights at your own pace.

Bike Rentals for Families

- If your kids are older, consider renting bikes through **Bike Share Toronto**. A **24-hour pass** costs **$7 CAD**, allowing unlimited 30-minute rides. There are bike paths along the waterfront and in parks like **High Park** and **Trinity Bellwoods**, making it easy and safe to explore the city by bike.

TTC Day Pass:
Cost: $13.50 CAD for unlimited rides (up to 5 children under 12 with

one adult)

Website: TTC Day Pass

How to get there: Available at subway stations and through the Presto app.

2. Budget-Friendly Attractions for Families

Toronto has plenty of free and low-cost attractions that are perfect for families. Many outdoor spaces, museums, and historical sites offer free or discounted admission for kids, making it easy to fill your itinerary without breaking the bank.

High Park

High Park (1873 Bloor St W) is a great spot for a family day out. It offers vast green spaces, walking trails, a free zoo, and playgrounds that kids will love. The park is especially beautiful in the spring when the cherry blossoms are in bloom, but it's a wonderful spot to explore year-round. Pack a picnic to enjoy at one of the many picnic tables, which can save you money on meals.

- **Location:** 1873 Bloor St W, Toronto, ON M6R 2Z3
- **Cost:** Free to enter, zoo is free
- **How to get there:** Take the **Line 2 subway** to **High Park Station**.

Toronto Islands

A ferry ride to the **Toronto Islands** is one of the most affordable and fun ways to spend a day with your family. The ferry ride itself offers great views of the Toronto skyline, and once you're on the islands, you can rent bikes, visit the playgrounds, and relax on the beaches. The **Centreville Amusement Park**, located on Centre Island, is perfect for younger kids, with rides costing around **$3-5 CAD** each.

- **Ferry Cost:** Round-trip ferry tickets are **$8.70 CAD** for adults, **$5.60 CAD** for seniors, and **$4.10 CAD** for children. Kids under 2 ride free.

- **How to get there:** Ferries depart from the **Jack Layton Ferry Terminal** at 9 Queens Quay W.

St. Lawrence Market

For a mix of history and delicious food, head to **St. Lawrence Market** (93 Front St E). While adults will enjoy browsing the market's vendors for artisanal foods and fresh produce, kids will love the bustling atmosphere. You can grab affordable snacks or a famous **peameal bacon sandwich** for about **$7-8 CAD**, which is a great way to feed the whole family on a budget.

- **Cost:** Free to enter
- **How to get there:** Take the **King streetcar** to **Jarvis St.**

Riverdale Farm

Riverdale Farm (201 Winchester St, Toronto, ON M4X 1B8) is another free attraction that's ideal for families with younger children. The farm is located in downtown Toronto and gives kids a chance to see farm animals up close, including sheep, cows, pigs, and chickens. There are also walking trails and picnic areas, making it easy to spend a few hours enjoying nature without spending a cent.

- **Location:** 201 Winchester St, Toronto, ON M4X 1B8
- **Cost:** Free
- **How to get there:** Take the **506 Carlton streetcar** to **Sumach St.**

3. Affordable Family Dining

Feeding a family on a budget doesn't have to be difficult in Toronto. The city offers a range of affordable dining options, from food markets to kid-friendly restaurants that won't strain your wallet.

Kensington Market

Kensington Market (Spadina Ave & Dundas St W) is the perfect spot for affordable, diverse meals. You can find everything from Mexican tacos to Caribbean jerk chicken, with most meals costing **$5-10 CAD**. It's a great place to grab a quick bite and let your kids try new foods without spending a lot.

- **Location:** Spadina Ave & Dundas St W, Toronto
- **How to get there:** Take the **Spadina streetcar** to Kensington Market.

Chinatown

Toronto's **Chinatown** (centered around Spadina Ave and Dundas St) is another great place for affordable family meals. You can find inexpensive dumplings, noodles, and other Asian dishes at restaurants like **Mother's Dumplings** (421 Spadina Ave), where a plate of dumplings costs around **$8-10 CAD**. It's a great option for a family meal that won't break the bank.

- **Location:** 421 Spadina Ave, Toronto, ON M5T 2G6
- **Cost:** Dumplings for **$8-10 CAD**
- **How to get there:** Take the **Spadina streetcar** to Dundas St.

Harbourfront Centre

If you're near the **Harbourfront**, grab a bite to eat at the nearby **Amsterdam Brewhouse** (245 Queens Quay W), which offers kid-friendly meals and views of Lake Ontario. They have a dedicated kids' menu with meals priced around **$7-10 CAD**, while adults can enjoy local brews and a wide range of food options at reasonable prices.

- **Location:** 245 Queens Quay W, Toronto, ON M5J 2K9
- **Cost:** Kids' meals for **$7-10 CAD**
- **How to get there:** Take the **509 Harbourfront streetcar** to Queens Quay W.

Food Trucks

In the summer months, Toronto has plenty of food trucks offering affordable, kid-friendly meals in parks and at public events. These trucks serve a wide range of foods, from burgers to ice cream, at reasonable prices. You can find food trucks at locations like **Nathan Phillips Square** and the **Toronto Islands**, where meals often cost around **$5-10 CAD**.

4. **Money-Saving Strategies for Attractions**

Toronto is home to many family-friendly attractions, but admission fees can add up. Here are some strategies to help you save on tickets and entry costs:

CityPass Toronto

If you're planning to visit several of Toronto's top attractions, such as the **CN Tower**, **Ripley's Aquarium**, or the **Royal Ontario Museum (ROM)**, consider purchasing a **Toronto CityPass**. The CityPass includes entry to five major attractions and costs **$104 CAD** for adults and **$78 CAD** for children. While this may seem like a bigger upfront cost, it saves you up to **40%** compared to buying individual tickets, especially if you're visiting multiple places with your family.

Free and Discount Days

Many of Toronto's museums and attractions offer free or discounted admission on certain days. For example, the **Royal Ontario Museum (ROM)** offers free admission to its permanent galleries on the third Monday of every month from **5:30 PM to 8:30 PM**. The **Art Gallery of Ontario (AGO)** is free on Wednesday evenings from **6:00 PM to 9:00 PM**. Keep an eye on museum websites for special promotions and free days.

Parks and Beaches

Toronto's public parks and beaches are free to access, making them perfect for a budget-friendly family day out. **Woodbine Beach** and **Cherry Beach** are great spots for swimming and picnicking in the summer, while parks like **High Park** and the **Toronto Islands** offer plenty of space for outdoor activities.

5. Packing Essentials for a Family Trip

To save money and avoid unnecessary expenses during your family trip to Toronto, it's important to pack the right essentials. Here are some tips on what to bring:

Reusable Water Bottles

Bring reusable water bottles for each family member. Toronto has clean, safe tap water, and there are water fountains throughout the city where you can refill your bottles for free. This will save you money on buying bottled water while keeping everyone hydrated during your day trips.

Snacks

Pack healthy snacks like granola bars, fruit, or crackers for your kids. Having snacks on hand can help you avoid impulse purchases at attractions, which tend to have higher-priced food options. If you're visiting a park or the Toronto Islands, pack a picnic to enjoy, which will save you even more on meals.

Sunscreen and Hats

If you're spending a lot of time outdoors, especially in the summer, be sure to pack sunscreen and hats for your kids. Toronto can get quite hot in the summer months, and sun protection is important. Buying sunscreen at convenience stores or attractions can be pricey, so bringing your own will save you money.

Comfortable Shoes

Toronto is a very walkable city, so make sure your kids have comfortable shoes. This will help you avoid the need for taxis or rideshares when walking becomes too much. Plus, walking is a great way to save money on transportation.

6. Customizing Your Itinerary for Families

Every family has different interests, so tailoring your itinerary to fit your family's preferences will make the trip more enjoyable. Here are a few ideas based on different types of family travelers:

For Active Families:

Spend a day biking around **Toronto Islands** or along the **Martin Goodman Trail**. You can rent bikes for the whole family at **Wheel Excitement** (249 Queens Quay W) for around **$12 CAD per hour**. Pack a picnic and enjoy lunch on one of the islands' beaches or parks.

For History Buff Families:

Visit the **Distillery District** and explore its historic cobblestone streets. Kids will enjoy the unique shops and public art, while adults can appreciate the Victorian-era architecture. Afterward, head to **Fort York** for a glimpse into Toronto's military history. Admission to Fort York is **$14 CAD** for adults and **$8 CAD** for kids.

For Nature-Loving Families:

Spend a day at **Rouge National Urban Park**, where you can hike the trails, spot wildlife, and enjoy a picnic in Canada's first national urban park. Admission is free, and it's a peaceful escape from the busy city.

Toronto for Solo Travelers

Safe and Affordable Neighborhoods for Solo Travelers

1. **Kensington Market**

Kensington Market is one of the most colorful and diverse neighborhoods in Toronto, perfect for solo travelers who want to experience local culture. This area is filled with vintage shops, street art, and affordable eateries, making it easy to explore on foot. Kensington Market is also close to other popular neighborhoods like **Chinatown** and **Queen Street West**, so you'll have plenty to see and do nearby.

Safety and Vibe:

- Kensington Market is generally safe during the day and early evening, though like any urban area, it's best to stay aware of your surroundings at night. The neighborhood has a laid-back, artsy vibe, and it's easy to strike up conversations with locals or other travelers.

Budget-Friendly Stays:

If you're looking for affordable accommodations, check out **Planet Traveler Hostel** (357 College St, Toronto, ON M5T 1S5). It's located right on the edge of Kensington Market and offers dorm rooms starting at around **$50 CAD per night**, with free breakfast and a rooftop lounge that's perfect for meeting other travelers. The hostel also organizes social events like movie nights and barbecues, which makes it easy to connect with others.

- **Location:** Kensington Market, Spadina Ave & Dundas St W
- **Cost:** Planet Traveler Hostel dorms from **$50 CAD per night**
- **How to get there:** Take the **Spadina streetcar** to Kensington Market.

2. **The Annex**

The **Annex** is a safe and affordable neighborhood popular with students and young professionals, thanks to its proximity to the **University of Toronto**. It's a lively area with plenty of budget-friendly restaurants, cafes, and shops, as well as easy access to public transportation. The Annex is also close to attractions like the **Royal Ontario Museum (ROM)** and **Queen's Park**, so there's always something to do nearby.

Safety and Vibe:

- The Annex is a very safe neighborhood, and it's busy day and night thanks to the student population. You'll find a good mix of affordable eateries, bookshops, and live music venues here. It's a great place to explore on foot, and it offers a local, laid-back atmosphere.

Budget-Friendly Stays:

- If you're looking for a place to stay, consider **The University of Toronto's New College Residences** (40 Willcocks St, Toronto, ON M5S 1C6), which rents out affordable rooms to travelers during the summer. Prices start around **$60 CAD per night**, and the location puts you within walking distance of many downtown attractions.
- **Location:** The Annex, around Bloor St W and Spadina Ave
- **Cost:** University of Toronto Residences from **$60 CAD per night**
- **How to get there:** Take the **Line 2 subway** to **Spadina Station**.

3. Queen Street West

Queen Street West is one of Toronto's trendiest neighborhoods, known for its mix of boutiques, cafes, and street art. Solo travelers will appreciate the area's lively atmosphere, with plenty of affordable options for dining and entertainment. It's also close to the **Entertainment District** and **Trinity Bellwoods Park**, making it easy to explore on foot or by public transport.

Safety and Vibe:

- Queen Street West is safe, particularly during the day and early evening. The area attracts a younger crowd and has a trendy, creative feel. There are always people out and about, so solo travelers will feel comfortable exploring on their own.

Budget-Friendly Stays:

Check out **The Drake Hotel** (1150 Queen St W, Toronto, ON M6J 1J3) for affordable boutique-style accommodations. While not the cheapest option in town, it's a great value for solo travelers looking for a cool, artsy vibe. Dorm rooms start around **$70 CAD per night**, and the hotel's rooftop bar is a great place to meet people.

- **Location:** Queen Street West, around Bathurst St and Ossington Ave
- **Cost:** Dorm rooms from **$70 CAD per night** at The Drake Hotel
- **How to get there:** Take the **501 Queen streetcar** west to **Dovercourt Rd.**

4. Downtown (Yonge-Dundas)

If you want to stay right in the heart of Toronto, **Downtown** around **Yonge-Dundas Square** is a great option for solo travelers. This area is close to many of Toronto's major attractions, including the **Eaton Centre**, **Nathan Phillips Square**, and the **Art Gallery of Ontario**. It's a safe and convenient spot for exploring the city, with lots of affordable dining options and easy access to public transportation.

Safety and Vibe:

Downtown Toronto is safe, though it's a busy area with lots of foot traffic. Solo travelers will feel comfortable walking around during the day and early evening, but like any downtown core, it's best to stay alert in more crowded areas at night.

Budget-Friendly Stays:

Consider staying at **HI Toronto Hostel** (76 Church St, Toronto, ON M5C 2G1), which offers dorm rooms starting at **$40 CAD per night**. The hostel is located just a short walk from **Yonge-Dundas Square** and organizes regular social events like pub crawls and city tours, making it easy to meet other travelers.

- **Location:** Yonge-Dundas Square, around Yonge St and Dundas St
- **Cost:** HI Toronto Hostel dorms from **$40 CAD per night**
- **How to get there:** Take the **Line 1 subway** to **Dundas Station**.

Meeting Other Travelers: Budget-Friendly Social Experiences

As a solo traveler, meeting people can be one of the highlights of your trip. Toronto offers plenty of budget-friendly social activities where you can connect with other travelers or locals, without spending too much. From hostel events to free meet-ups, there are many ways to make friends and have fun.

1. Hostel Events

Staying at a hostel is one of the easiest ways to meet fellow travelers. Many hostels in Toronto organize social events like pub crawls, movie nights, and walking tours that are either free or very affordable. These events give you a chance to connect with others in a laid-back setting, and you'll often find other solo travelers to join you on your adventures.

HI Toronto Hostel Pub Crawls

HI Toronto Hostel (76 Church St) regularly organizes pub crawls, which are a great way to experience the city's nightlife while meeting other travelers. The pub crawls typically cost around **$10 CAD** and include visits to local bars and pubs where you can grab a drink and chat with people from all over the world.

Planet Traveler Hostel Social Events

Planet Traveler Hostel (357 College St) offers a variety of free social events for guests, including movie nights, rooftop barbecues, and trivia nights. These events are perfect for solo travelers who want to meet others in a more relaxed, communal setting. The hostel's rooftop patio also offers amazing views of the city, and it's a great spot to unwind and socialize.

2. Free Walking Tours

Another great way to meet people and explore the city on a budget is by joining a **free walking tour**. These tours are often led by local guides who show you around different neighborhoods while sharing interesting stories about Toronto's history and culture. While the tours are free, it's customary to tip the guide if you enjoy the experience.

Tour Guys Toronto

Tour Guys offers free walking tours of Toronto, with different routes that cover areas like the **Entertainment District**, **Chinatown**, and **Kensington Market**. The tours typically last around two hours and are a great way to meet other solo travelers while getting to know the city.

- **Website:** Tour Guys Toronto
- **Cost:** Free (tips appreciated)

3. **Meetup.com Groups**

Toronto has a large and active community on **Meetup.com**, with groups for just about every interest. Joining a **meetup** is a great way to meet locals and other travelers with similar interests, whether you're into hiking, photography, food, or board games.

Budget Tip:

Many meetup groups offer free or low-cost activities, such as hiking in **High Park** or playing board games at a local café. Check out the events section of Meetup.com to find budget-friendly activities happening during your stay.

- **Website:** Meetup Toronto

4. **Local Pubs and Cafes**

If you're more of an introvert or prefer a quieter atmosphere, heading to a local pub or café is a great way to meet people without the need for organized events. Toronto has plenty of welcoming spots where solo travelers can strike up a conversation with locals or fellow tourists.

The Rex Hotel Jazz & Blues Bar

The Rex Hotel Jazz & Blues Bar (194 Queen St W) is a laid-back venue where you can enjoy live jazz and blues performances every night of the week. The cover charge is usually around **$10-15 CAD**, and the intimate atmosphere makes it easy to chat with other music lovers.

- **Location:** 194 Queen St W, Toronto, ON M5V 1Z1
- **Cost:** Cover charge **$10-15 CAD**
- **How to get there:** Take the **501 Queen streetcar** to Queen St W.

Snakes & Lattes Board Game Café

If you're looking for a fun way to spend an evening, head to **Snakes & Lattes** (600 Bloor St W, Toronto, ON M6G 1K4), a board game café where you can play games and meet other travelers or locals. It's a great place to hang out solo or join a group for a few rounds of games. The cover charge is around **$8 CAD**, which includes access to a wide selection of board games.

- **Location:** 600 Bloor St W, Toronto, ON M6G 1K4
- **Cost: $8 CAD** cover charge for games
- **How to get there:** Take the **Line 2 subway** to **Bathurst Station**.

5. **Outdoor Events and Festivals**

Toronto hosts numerous free outdoor events and festivals throughout the year, many of which are perfect for solo travelers looking to meet people and enjoy the local culture.

Kensington Market Pedestrian Sundays

On the last Sunday of every month from May to October, **Kensington Market** becomes a pedestrian-only zone filled with live music, street performers, and food stalls. It's a lively event where you can wander the streets, grab some street food, and chat with locals or other travelers. The event is free to attend, making it a great budget-friendly option.

- **Location:** Kensington Market, Spadina Ave & Dundas St W
- **Cost:** Free
- **How to get there:** Take the **Spadina streetcar** to Kensington Market.

Harbourfront Centre Events

Harbourfront Centre (235 Queens Quay W) hosts free cultural events and performances throughout the year, including live music, dance performances, and outdoor film screenings. It's a great place to mingle with locals and enjoy the vibrant waterfront atmosphere without spending any money.

- **Location:** 235 Queens Quay W, Toronto, ON M5J 2G8
- **Cost:** Free
- **How to get there:** Take the **509 Harbourfront streetcar** to Queens Quay W.

Best Hostels for Solo Adventurers

Staying in a hostel is not only budget-friendly, but it's also a great way for solo travelers to meet new people and share travel stories. Toronto's hostels are known for their friendly atmospheres, safety features, and excellent locations, making them ideal for solo adventurers.

1. **The Planet Traveler Hostel**

   The Planet Traveler Hostel (357 College St, Toronto, ON M5T 1S5) is one of the most popular hostels in Toronto, especially for solo travelers. Located in the heart of **Kensington Market**, this eco-friendly hostel offers a mix of dorms and private rooms at affordable prices. The social atmosphere makes it easy to meet other travelers, and they often organize activities like movie nights and pub crawls.

   - **Safety Features:** The hostel has 24-hour security, lockers for personal belongings, and keycard access to rooms, which makes it a safe choice for solo travelers.
   - **Social Environment:** The rooftop terrace with views of the CN Tower is a great place to hang out with other guests. They also offer a free breakfast, which is a perfect way to start your day while meeting fellow travelers.
   - **Price:** Dorm beds start at around **$40 CAD per night**, while private rooms are priced at around **$100 CAD**.
   - **Location:** Planet Traveler Hostel 357 College St, Toronto, ON M5T 1S5
   - **Cost:** Dorms from **$40 CAD**, private rooms from **$100 CAD**

- **How to get there:** Take the **506 Carlton streetcar** to **College St & Augusta Ave.**

2. HI Toronto Hostel

HI Toronto Hostel (76 Church St, Toronto, ON M5C 2G1) is a part of the **Hostelling International** network and offers a vibrant social atmosphere that's perfect for solo travelers. Located in the downtown core, this hostel is within walking distance of many major attractions, including the **St. Lawrence Market** and the **Distillery District**.

- **Safety Features:** The hostel offers 24-hour front desk service, secure lockers, and keycard access for all rooms, ensuring that solo travelers feel safe and secure during their stay.
- **Social Environment:** HI Toronto is known for its lively communal spaces, including **The Cavern Bar** located in the basement. The bar hosts events like trivia nights and live music, providing a fun way to meet people. They also organize walking tours and other activities for guests.
- **Price:** Dorm beds start at around **$45 CAD per night**, and private rooms are available from **$110 CAD**.
- **Location:** HI Toronto Hostel 76 Church St, Toronto, ON M5C 2G1
- **Cost:** Dorms from **$45 CAD**, private rooms from **$110 CAD**
- **How to get there:** Take the **King streetcar** to **Church St.**

3. The Clarence Park

Located in the **Entertainment District**, **The Clarence Park** (7 Clarence Square, Toronto, ON M5V 1H1) is a cozy boutique-style hostel with a friendly atmosphere and a great location. It's a smaller, quieter option compared to some of the larger hostels, making it ideal for solo travelers looking for a bit more privacy.

- **Safety Features:** The hostel offers secure lockers, keycard access, and 24-hour front desk service, ensuring a safe stay.
- **Social Environment:** The Clarence Park has a relaxed vibe, with a shared kitchen and outdoor patio where you can chat with fellow travelers over breakfast or a drink. It's close to major attractions like the **CN Tower** and **Rogers Centre**, making it easy to explore the city.
- **Price:** Dorm beds start at **$35 CAD per night**, and private rooms start at around **$90 CAD**.
- **Location:** The Clarence Park 7 Clarence Square, Toronto, ON M5V 1H1
- **Cost:** Dorms from **$35 CAD**, private rooms from **$90 CAD**
- **How to get there:** Take the **King streetcar** to **Spadina Ave** and walk west to Clarence Square.

4. **The Only Backpacker's Inn**

Located in Toronto's **Greektown**, **The Only Backpacker's Inn** (966 Danforth Ave, Toronto, ON M4J 1L9) is a laid-back hostel that offers an affordable and social experience for solo travelers. It's further from the downtown core, but well-connected by public transit, and the neighborhood offers a more local experience.

- **Safety Features:** The hostel provides secure lockers, 24-hour front desk service, and keycard access to rooms.
- **Social Environment:** The Only Backpacker's Inn has a lively bar and café attached to the hostel, and they organize social events like trivia nights and open mic sessions. The hostel also has a garden patio where guests can relax and chat with each other.
- **Price:** Dorm beds start at around **$30 CAD per night**, and private rooms are available from **$80 CAD**.
- **Location:** The Only Backpacker's Inn, 966 Danforth Ave, Toronto, ON M4J 1L9
- **Cost:** Dorms from **$30 CAD**, private rooms from **$80 CAD**

- **How to get there:** Take the **Line 2 subway** to **Donlands Station** and walk to Danforth Ave.

Cheap Cafés and Bars for Solo Dining

1. Jimmy's Coffee

If you're looking for a laid-back café where you can enjoy a quiet coffee and get some work done, **Jimmy's Coffee** is a great choice. With several locations across the city, Jimmy's offers a cozy atmosphere with plenty of seating for solo travelers. The café is known for its smooth coffee blends and friendly staff.

- **Why It's Great for Solo Travelers:** Jimmy's is perfect for solo diners who want a relaxed environment to enjoy a coffee or light snack. The café is welcoming to people who want to sit with a laptop or a book for a while, and the casual vibe makes it easy to feel at home.
- **Menu:** Coffee starts at **$3 CAD**, and they offer a variety of pastries and snacks for around **$4-7 CAD**.
- **Location:** Jimmy's Coffee (Multiple Locations) 107 Portland St, Toronto, ON M5V 2N3 (flagship location)
- **Cost:** Coffee from **$3 CAD**, snacks from **$4 CAD**
- **How to get there:** Take the **501 Queen streetcar** to **Portland St**.

2. Early Bird Café

For a modern and trendy café with a focus on affordable, high-quality coffee and light meals, head to **Early Bird Café** (613 Queen St W, Toronto, ON M5V 2B7). Located in the heart of Queen West, it's a perfect stop for solo travelers looking to enjoy a coffee and people-watch.

- **Why It's Great for Solo Travelers:** The bright and airy atmosphere is ideal for solo diners, with plenty of space to relax. Whether you're grabbing a coffee to go or sitting down for a light lunch, you'll find it easy to enjoy some quiet time here.

- **Menu:** Coffee starts at **$3.50 CAD**, and they offer sandwiches and salads for around **$8-12 CAD**.
- **Location:** Early Bird Café 613 Queen St W, Toronto, ON M5V 2B7
- **Cost:** Coffee from **$3.50 CAD**, meals from **$8 CAD**
- **How to get there:** Take the **501 Queen streetcar** to **Bathurst St**.

3. **The Green Beanery**

The Green Beanery (565 Bloor St W, Toronto, ON M5S 1Y6) is an eco-conscious café that offers affordable coffee and snacks in a casual environment. The café is known for supporting ethical sourcing and sustainable practices, making it a great option for environmentally-conscious solo travelers.

- **Why It's Great for Solo Travelers:** The spacious interior and free Wi-Fi make it a great spot to relax or work on your laptop. It's a popular spot for students and locals, so you'll blend right in whether you're grabbing a coffee or spending an afternoon there.
- **Menu:** Coffee starts at **$2.50 CAD**, and they offer a range of pastries and sandwiches for around **$4-7 CAD**.
- **Location:** The Green Beanery, 565 Bloor St W, Toronto, ON M5S 1Y6
- **Cost:** Coffee from **$2.50 CAD**, snacks from **$4 CAD**
- **How to get there:** Take the **Line 2 subway** to **Bathurst Station**.

4. **The Only Café**

Attached to **The Only Backpacker's Inn**, **The Only Café** (966 Danforth Ave, Toronto, ON M4J 1L9) is a lively bar and café that's perfect for solo travelers looking for an affordable drink or snack. It has a relaxed, community feel and often hosts live music or trivia nights, which makes it easy to strike up a conversation with locals.

- **Why It's Great for Solo Travelers:** The friendly, informal atmosphere of The Only Café makes it a great spot for solo diners. The communal seating encourages interaction, but there are also quieter corners if you just want to enjoy your meal solo.
- **Menu:** They offer a wide range of craft beers starting at **$5-7 CAD**, and light meals like sandwiches and salads for around **$8-12 CAD**.
- **Location:** The Only Café 966 Danforth Ave, Toronto, ON M4J 1L9
- **Cost:** Craft beers from **$5 CAD**, meals from **$8 CAD**
- **How to get there:** Take the **Line 2 subway** to **Donlands Station**.

5. **Sneaky Dee's**

Sneaky Dee's (431 College St, Toronto, ON M5T 1T1) is a popular Tex-Mex spot in Toronto that's great for solo travelers looking for a lively atmosphere and affordable eats. Known for its huge portions and laid-back vibe, it's a go-to spot for cheap, filling meals.

- **Why It's Great for Solo Travelers:** The casual, no-frills vibe makes it easy to feel comfortable dining solo. The staff is friendly, and it's a great place to grab a quick bite before exploring the nearby Kensington Market.
- **Menu:** A plate of nachos costs about **$12-15 CAD**, and they offer tacos, burritos, and other Tex-Mex staples for around **$8-12 CAD**.
- **Location:** Sneaky Dee's 431 College St, Toronto, ON M5T 1T1
- **Cost:** Meals from **$8-15 CAD**
- **How to get there:** Take the **506 Carlton streetcar** to **College St & Bathurst St**.

Solo Travel Safety Tips for Toronto

1. Use Public Transportation Safely

Toronto's public transportation system, the **TTC (Toronto Transit Commission)**, is a reliable and affordable way to get around the city. As a solo traveler, it's important to be aware of your surroundings and follow basic safety tips while using buses, streetcars, and subways.

Stick to well-lit, busy stations:

Most subway stations in Toronto are well-lit and have a lot of foot traffic, especially in the downtown core. Try to stick to busy stations like **Union Station, Bloor-Yonge,** and **St. George**, where there are always people around. Late at night, avoid isolated stations or dark platforms.

Sit near the driver or conductor:

When using the bus or streetcar at night, it's a good idea to sit near the front, close to the driver or conductor. This ensures that you're in a more visible and safer area. TTC vehicles are equipped with cameras, so the drivers can see what's happening inside the bus or streetcar.

Budget Tip:

Consider using a **TTC Day Pass** if you're planning to make multiple trips in a day. For **$13.50 CAD**, you get unlimited rides for the entire day, which can help you explore the city while saving money on transportation.

TTC Day Pass:

- **Cost: $13.50 CAD** for unlimited daily rides
- **Where to buy:** Available at TTC stations and through the Presto app
- **How to get there:** Available at subway stations

2. Stay in Safe and Affordable Neighborhoods

When traveling alone, it's important to choose your accommodations in a safe and central area. Toronto has plenty of budget-friendly neighborhoods that are not only affordable but also secure and well-connected to public transportation.

Safe Neighborhoods for Solo Travelers:

- **Downtown Toronto (Entertainment District, Queen Street West, and Harbourfront):** These areas are filled with restaurants, cafes, and attractions that are perfect for solo travelers. They're safe to walk around during the day and night, and you'll always find other people around.
- **Kensington Market:** A lively and eclectic neighborhood, Kensington Market is a great place for solo travelers looking for a budget-friendly area with lots of character. It's a very walkable neighborhood with plenty of cafes and independent shops.
- **The Annex:** Located near the University of Toronto, this neighborhood is home to students, young professionals, and solo travelers alike. The area is safe, filled with affordable cafes, and close to the subway for easy access to other parts of the city.

Budget Tip:

Consider staying in a hostel or guesthouse where you can meet other solo travelers. **HI Toronto Hostel** (76 Church St, Toronto, ON M5C 2G1) is centrally located and offers budget-friendly dormitory rooms starting at **$40-50 CAD** per night. Not only will you save money, but you'll also have the chance to connect with other travelers who may be exploring the city solo as well.

HI Toronto Hostel:

- **Cost:** Dorm rooms starting at **$40 CAD** per night
- **Location:** 76 Church St, Toronto, ON M5C 2G1

- **How to get there:** Take the **504 King streetcar** or walk from **King Station**.

3. Be Smart When Walking at Night

Toronto is generally safe to walk around, even at night, but it's always wise to take a few precautions when you're exploring the city alone after dark.

Stick to busy, well-lit streets:

When walking at night, stay on streets that are well-lit and have plenty of foot traffic. Main streets like **Queen Street West, Yonge Street**, and the **Entertainment District** are good places to walk in the evening. If you're unsure about the safety of a particular area, ask a local or a staff member at your accommodation.

Avoid secluded parks or alleys at night:

While parks like **Trinity Bellwoods** and **High Park** are great to visit during the day, they can be very quiet and empty at night. It's best to avoid walking through these areas alone after dark, and instead stick to busier parts of the city.

Budget Tip:

If you're walking late at night and don't feel comfortable, use a rideshare app like **Uber** or **Lyft** for a quick and affordable ride back to your accommodation. Short rides within downtown Toronto typically cost **$10-15 CAD**, which is a reasonable price for peace of mind.

Uber:

- **Cost:** Rides within downtown Toronto typically cost **$10-15 CAD**
- **How to get there:** Download the Uber app to request a ride.

4. Keep Your Valuables Secure

When traveling alone, it's essential to keep your belongings safe and secure, especially in crowded areas or on public transportation. Toronto is generally safe, but pickpocketing and petty theft can happen in busy tourist spots.

Use a crossbody bag or money belt:
Keep your valuables close by wearing a crossbody bag with zippers, or use a money belt to store cash, credit cards, and your passport. This will make it more difficult for someone to steal from you in crowded areas like **Yonge-Dundas Square** or on the subway.

Avoid flashing expensive items:
While Toronto is a safe city, it's always best to avoid drawing attention to expensive items like jewelry, high-end cameras, or gadgets. Keep your phone and wallet in a secure place when not in use, and be discreet with your valuables.

Budget Tip:
Leave unnecessary valuables, such as extra credit cards or your passport, in a secure locker at your accommodation or use a travel safe. This will reduce the risk of theft while you're out exploring the city.

5. Solo Dining: Eating Out Safely and Comfortably

Dining alone in Toronto is a pleasant experience, with many cafes, restaurants, and markets that cater to solo travelers. If you're unsure about where to eat or want to save some money while still enjoying good food, Toronto offers a variety of safe and affordable options.

Try Cafes with Communal Seating:
Many cafes in Toronto, such as **Dark Horse Espresso Bar** (215 Spadina Ave, Toronto, ON M5T 2C7), offer communal tables where solo travelers can comfortably eat or work. You'll often find other people doing the same, and it's a great way to enjoy a meal without feeling awkward dining alone.

- **Location:** 215 Spadina Ave, Toronto, ON M5T 2C7
- **Cost:** Coffee and pastries for around **$5-10 CAD**
- **How to get there:** Take the **510 Spadina streetcar** to Queen St W.

Head to Kensington Market for Casual Dining:

Kensington Market is a perfect place for solo travelers looking for casual and affordable dining options. You can find food stalls and small restaurants offering a wide range of international cuisines, with most meals costing **$5-10 CAD**. The relaxed atmosphere makes it easy to grab a bite to eat on your own without standing out.

- **Location:** Spadina Ave & Dundas St W, Toronto
- **How to get there:** Take the **510 Spadina streetcar** to Kensington Market.
- **Visit St. Lawrence Market for a Solo Meal:**

St. Lawrence Market (93 Front St E) is a great place for solo travelers to grab a meal while exploring one of Toronto's most famous food markets. You can pick up affordable sandwiches, snacks, and fresh produce, and there are seating areas where you can eat while people-watching. Meals like the famous **peameal bacon sandwich** cost about **$7-8 CAD**.

- **Location:** 93 Front St E, Toronto
- **Cost:** Meals for **$7-10 CAD**
- **How to get there:** Take the **King streetcar** to **Jarvis St.**

6. Meet Other Travelers Safely

Solo travel doesn't have to mean being alone all the time. Toronto is full of opportunities to meet other travelers, whether you're staying in a hostel, joining a walking tour, or attending local events. Here are some safe ways to connect with others while exploring the city.

Stay in Social Accommodations:

Hostels like **The Planet Traveler** (357 College St, Toronto, ON M5T 1S5) offer social atmospheres where solo travelers can meet others in a safe environment. The hostel organizes group activities, such as pub crawls and walking tours, which are great for connecting with fellow travelers.

- **Cost:** Dorm rooms starting at **$45 CAD** per night
- **How to get there:** Take the **506 Carlton streetcar** to College St.

Join a Free Walking Tour:

- Many organizations offer free walking tours of Toronto, which are perfect for solo travelers looking to explore the city while meeting new people. **Tour Guys** offers free tours of downtown Toronto, the **Distillery District**, and other neighborhoods. These tours are led by knowledgeable guides and provide a safe way to explore the city in a group setting.
- **Cost:** Free (tips are encouraged)
- **How to get there:** Tours start at various locations; check the **Tour Guys** website for details.

Attend Local Events and Meetups:

- If you're looking to meet locals and other solo travelers, check out events and meetups happening around Toronto. Websites like **Meetup.com** list events ranging from hiking groups to language exchanges. It's a safe and structured way to meet people with similar interests.

Money-Saving Tips

Finding Discounts and Coupons for Attractions

1. City Passes: The Ultimate Attraction Discount

If you plan on visiting several major attractions in Toronto, buying a **CityPass** is one of the best ways to save money. This pass bundles admission to five top attractions, saving you up to 40% compared to buying tickets separately.

Toronto CityPass

The **Toronto CityPass** includes entry to the **CN Tower**, **Ripley's Aquarium**, the **Royal Ontario Museum (ROM)**, **Casa Loma**, and the **Toronto Zoo** or **Ontario Science Centre**. For **$104 CAD** for adults and **$78 CAD** for children, this pass covers multiple must-see attractions at a significant discount.

Budget Tip:

The CityPass is valid for 9 days from the first use, giving you plenty of time to visit each attraction at your own pace. If you plan your visits over several days, you can spread out the cost and fully enjoy each experience.

Toronto CityPass:

- **Cost: $104 CAD** for adults, **$78 CAD** for children

- **How to get there:** Purchase online at Toronto CityPass or at any of the participating attractions.

2. Groupon Deals: Discounts on Local Attractions and Activities

Groupon is a popular platform where you can find discounted tickets for many local attractions, tours, and activities in Toronto. It's a great way to save money on experiences that may not be included in other discount passes.

How to Use Groupon:

Simply visit **Groupon's Toronto page** and search for deals on attractions, restaurants, tours, and other activities. You'll often find discounts ranging from 10-50% off regular prices. For example, you might come across deals for walking tours, museum passes, or even boat cruises at a fraction of the usual price.

Budget Tip:

Groupon often has limited-time offers, so check the site regularly before your trip to see what's available. Make sure to read the fine print on expiration dates and blackout periods before purchasing.

Groupon Toronto:
Website: Groupon Toronto

3. Tourism Websites: Access Exclusive Deals and Packages

Local tourism websites are a great resource for finding discounts, promotions, and special offers on attractions and events. These sites often partner with local businesses and attractions to provide travelers with the best deals.

Destination Toronto:

- The official tourism website, **Destination Toronto**, regularly lists

promotions and offers for visitors. You can find discounted tickets, attraction packages, and seasonal deals on the site. It's also a good place to discover lesser-known attractions that might not be included in other discount programs.
- **Website:** Destination Toronto

Budget Tip:

- Many hotels in Toronto also offer **stay-and-play** packages, where you can book accommodations that include discounted or free tickets to attractions like the CN Tower or Ripley's Aquarium. Check the **special offers** section on the Destination Toronto website for these deals.

4. **Free Attractions and Donation-Based Entry**

Toronto has many free or donation-based attractions, making it easy to enjoy the city's culture and history without spending much. Here are a few notable spots where you can explore for little to no cost:

- **Art Gallery of Ontario (AGO):** Free admission to the permanent collection on Wednesday evenings from **6:00 PM to 9:00 PM**.
- **Royal Ontario Museum (ROM):** Free admission to the permanent galleries on the third Monday of every month from **5:30 PM to 8:30 PM**.
- **St. Lawrence Market:** Free to enter and explore, with plenty of affordable food options.
- **Riverdale Farm:** A free urban farm where families can see farm animals and explore the surrounding park.

Art Gallery of Ontario (AGO):

- **Location:** 317 Dundas St W, Toronto, ON M5T 1G4

- **Cost:** Free on Wednesdays from **6:00 PM to 9:00 PM**
- **How to get there:** Take the **505 Dundas streetcar** to McCaul St.

5. Coupon Books and Flyers

Another way to save on Toronto attractions is by picking up local coupon books or flyers, often available at tourist information centers, hotels, and major transit hubs like **Union Station**.

Attraction Coupons:

- Many of these coupon books include **2-for-1 deals** or **10-20% discounts** on popular attractions, tours, and dining options. These physical coupons are an easy way to save, especially if you're traveling in a group or with family.

Budget Tip:

- Look for coupon stands at **Union Station**, major tourist areas like **Yonge-Dundas Square**, and even in hotel lobbies. They often contain valuable discounts that can be used throughout your trip.

How to Score Cheap Tickets to Major Events

1. Last-Minute Deals and Apps

Several apps and websites offer discounted tickets to events that haven't sold out, particularly for last-minute bookings. This is a great way to get affordable tickets to concerts, theater shows, and sporting events.

TodayTix:

TodayTix offers discounted theater tickets to shows in Toronto, including

Mirvish Productions performances. You can find same-day and next-day tickets at up to 50% off. It's easy to use—just download the app, browse available shows, and purchase tickets directly.

- **Website:** TodayTix

Budget Tip: Check the app daily for flash sales and rush tickets, where prices drop significantly a few hours before showtime.

SeatGeek:
SeatGeek is another platform that allows you to search for discounted tickets to concerts, sports games, and events in Toronto. You can compare prices from different sellers and find the best deals for the seats you want. Prices often drop as the event date approaches, so it's worth checking the app regularly if you're flexible with your plans.

- **Website:** SeatGeek

Budget Tip: Use promo codes that are frequently available on the app for new users to get an extra discount on your first purchase.

2. **Rush Tickets and Lottery Systems for Theater Shows**
For theater lovers, Toronto has several ways to access affordable tickets through rush ticket programs and lotteries.

Mirvish Rush Tickets:
Mirvish Productions, which runs some of Toronto's biggest theater shows, offers rush tickets for same-day performances at a significantly reduced price. You can buy these tickets at the box office starting at **9:00 AM** on the day of the show, with prices as low as **$29-49 CAD** depending on the production. It's a first-come, first-served system, so getting there early increases your chances of snagging a deal.

- **Website:** Mirvish Rush Tickets
- **Location:** Various theaters, including the **Princess of Wales Theatre** and **Royal Alexandra Theatre**.

Budget Tip:
Follow **Mirvish Productions** on social media to stay updated on rush ticket availability and special promotions. They often post when tickets go on sale, making it easier to plan.

3. **Student and Youth Discounts**
If you're a student or under 30, there are additional discounts available for various events in Toronto. Always carry a student ID or check websites for youth pricing.

T.O. Tix:
T.O. Tix is Toronto's official one-stop shop for discounted theater and event tickets. They offer same-day and last-minute tickets at reduced prices, often with special discounts for students. You can browse online or visit their booth in **Yonge-Dundas Square** to check out available tickets.

- **Website:** T.O. Tix
- **Location:** Yonge-Dundas Square, 1 Dundas St E, Toronto

4. **Group Tickets for Sports Events**
If you're attending a sporting event like a **Toronto Blue Jays** game or a **Toronto Raptors** match, buying group tickets can help reduce the cost per person. Many teams offer discounted rates for groups of **10 or more**, making it an affordable option if you're traveling with friends or family.

Toronto Blue Jays Group Tickets:
You can get group discounts for **Blue Jays** games at the **Rogers Centre**, with savings depending on the size of your group and the section you choose.

Group tickets typically start at **$20 CAD** per person, making it a fun and affordable way to enjoy a baseball game.

- **Website:** Toronto Blue Jays
- **Location:** Rogers Centre, 1 Blue Jays Way, Toronto

Budget Tip:
Check for **special promotion days**, such as **$1 Hot Dog Nights** or **Fan Appreciation Days**, where you can save even more on food and souvenirs.

5. **Free and Low-Cost Local Events**

Toronto hosts a wide range of free and low-cost events throughout the year, from outdoor concerts and festivals to street fairs and cultural celebrations. Many of these events are perfect for budget-conscious travelers who want to experience the city's vibrant cultural scene without spending much.

Toronto Music Garden:

During the summer months, the **Toronto Music Garden** at Harbourfront hosts free classical music performances and concerts. It's a peaceful and scenic venue, making it a great way to enjoy live music outdoors.

- **Location:** 479 Queens Quay W, Toronto, ON M5V 2Y3
- **Cost:** Free
- **How to get there:** Take the **509 Harbourfront streetcar** to Queens Quay W.

Toronto Outdoor Art Fair:

Held annually in **Nathan Phillips Square**, the **Toronto Outdoor Art Fair** is a free event where you can explore works from local and international artists. It's one of the best opportunities to experience Toronto's arts scene without spending a dime.

- **Location:** 100 Queen St W, Toronto, ON M5H 2N1

- **Cost:** Free
- **How to get there:** Take the **Line 1 subway** to Queen Station.

Budget Tip Summary

- **Use Toronto CityPass** for major attractions and save up to 40%.
- **Groupon** offers daily discounts on local attractions, tours, and restaurants.
- **Tourism websites** like **Destination Toronto** provide exclusive deals and seasonal promotions.
- Check out **free attractions** like the **Art Gallery of Ontario (AGO)** and **Riverdale Farm**.
- Use apps like **TodayTix** and **SeatGeek** for last-minute event deals and affordable tickets.
- Attend **free events** like concerts at **Harbourfront** or art fairs at **Nathan Phillips Square**.
- Take advantage of **group tickets** for sporting events to lower costs per person.

Budget Travel Apps You Need in Toronto

1. **TTC Watch – Toronto Bus and Streetcar Tracker**

The **TTC Watch** app is essential for getting around Toronto on a budget. It provides real-time updates on bus, streetcar, and subway schedules, helping you plan your trips efficiently without relying on taxis or ride-hailing services. Using public transportation is one of the best ways to save money in Toronto, and this app makes it easier by showing you the nearest TTC routes and expected arrival times.

Key Features:

- Real-time tracking of buses, streetcars, and subways.
- Provides notifications for delays or service changes.
- Allows you to save your favorite routes for quick access.

Budget Tip:

- Combine the **TTC Watch** app with a **TTC Day Pass** (available for **$13.50 CAD**) to get unlimited rides for the day, making it easier to explore the city without overspending on transportation.

App Cost: Free
Where to get it: Available on the **App Store** and **Google Play**.

2. **Too Good To Go – Save on Food**

Food can be one of the biggest expenses while traveling, but **Too Good To Go** helps you find heavily discounted meals from restaurants, bakeries, and cafes that have surplus food at the end of the day. You can purchase meals or snacks at a fraction of the original price, helping you eat well on a budget while reducing food waste.

Key Features:

- Find deals on meals at local restaurants, cafes, and bakeries.
- Prices are usually 50% or more off the regular price.
- Discover new places to eat while saving money.

Budget Tip:

- Check the app in the late afternoon or early evening for the best deals. You can often find meals for as low as **$5-8 CAD** that would otherwise be much more expensive.

App Cost: Free

Where to get it: Available on the **App Store** and **Google Play**.

3. UberEats – Use Promo Codes for Discounts

While **UberEats** is widely known for food delivery, it's also a great tool for budget travelers if you use promo codes and take advantage of deals offered by the app. Toronto is filled with affordable eateries, and with UberEats, you can often find discounts on delivery or pickup orders, especially if you're a new user or if there's a special promotion going on.

Key Features:

- Access exclusive discounts on local restaurants.
- Offers deals for new users and ongoing promotions.
- Pickup option allows you to skip delivery fees.

Budget Tip:

- Keep an eye out for promo codes, which can often save you **$5-10 CAD** off your first few orders. You can also filter by "deals" to find special offers from restaurants.

App Cost: Free

Where to get it: Available on the **App Store** and **Google Play**.

4. HotelTonight – Last-Minute Deals on Accommodations

If you're flexible with your accommodation plans, **HotelTonight** is an excellent app for finding last-minute deals on hotels in Toronto. The app lists unsold hotel rooms at discounted prices, sometimes offering up to **50% off** the original room rate. It's ideal for budget travelers who are open to spontaneity or looking for an affordable place to stay at short notice.

Key Features:

Find discounted hotel rooms for same-day or last-minute bookings.

- Curated list of quality hotels, from budget-friendly options to more luxurious stays.
- Offers exclusive deals that are not available on other platforms.

Budget Tip:
If you're visiting Toronto during off-peak times or weekdays, you're more likely to find great discounts on HotelTonight. Prices typically drop in the late afternoon or evening for same-day bookings.
App Cost: Free
Where to get it: Available on the **App Store** and **Google Play**.

5. **Skyscanner – Flights and Transportation**
Though known for helping travelers find cheap flights, **Skyscanner** also offers deals on car rentals and buses in Toronto. The app allows you to compare prices across different airlines, bus services, and car rentals, so you can choose the most affordable options for getting around the city or traveling to nearby areas.

Key Features:

- Search and compare prices for flights, car rentals, and buses.
- Offers flexible date options to help you find the cheapest travel days.
- Find last-minute deals on transportation.

Budget Tip:

- Use Skyscanner to find the best deal on a rental car if you're planning day trips outside Toronto, like to **Niagara Falls** or **Algonquin Park**.

App Cost: Free
Where to get it: Available on the **App Store** and **Google Play**.

Best Websites for Deals on Food, Entertainment, and Stays

1. Groupon – Discounts on Activities, Dining, and Entertainment

Groupon is one of the best websites for finding deals on everything from dining to entertainment in Toronto. Whether you want to go out for a meal, book a tour, or visit an attraction, Groupon offers significant discounts that can save you up to **50% or more** on regular prices.

What You Can Find:

- Discounts on restaurants, cafes, and food experiences.
- Deals on local attractions like the **CN Tower** or **Ripley's Aquarium**.
- Savings on fitness classes, spa treatments, and more.

Budget Tip:

- Always check Groupon before booking any tours or activities in Toronto. You can often find "Buy One Get One Free" deals or up to **50% off** on admission to popular attractions.

Website: Groupon Toronto

2. TravelZoo – Travel and Dining Deals

TravelZoo offers curated deals for both tourists and locals, including discounts on hotels, dining, tours, and entertainment. It's a great resource for budget travelers looking for exclusive offers on experiences in Toronto, often featuring flash sales and limited-time deals.

What You Can Find:

- Discounted hotel packages, sometimes including meals or extras like

parking.
- Deals on local restaurants, often with set menus or discounts on food and drinks.
- Reduced rates for shows, events, and seasonal festivals.

Budget Tip:

- Sign up for the TravelZoo newsletter to get notifications about special sales and flash deals, which often provide limited-time discounts on hotels and dining experiences.

Website: TravelZoo Toronto

3. Booking.com – Best for Accommodation Deals

Booking.com is one of the best websites for budget travelers looking for affordable accommodation in Toronto. The platform frequently offers deals and discounts, especially if you book in advance or have flexible travel dates. Booking.com also provides reviews and ratings from other travelers, so you can make sure you're getting good value for your money.

What You Can Find:

- Discounts on hotels, guesthouses, and hostels.
- Exclusive deals for **Genius members** (free sign-up) with up to **10% off** select properties.
- Flexible cancellation policies, which are useful for budget travelers who need to adjust plans.

Budget Tip:

- Look for last-minute deals or free cancellation policies. Sometimes, you can book a hotel at a discounted rate and still cancel if you find a better deal elsewhere closer to your travel date.

Website: Booking.com

4. BlogTO – Local Events and Free Activities

BlogTO is a local website that covers everything happening in Toronto, from food and entertainment to news and events. For budget travelers, BlogTO is a goldmine of information on free activities, cheap eats, and local events that won't cost much.

What You Can Find:

- Listings for free concerts, street festivals, and public events happening around the city.
- Reviews of affordable restaurants, food trucks, and cafes.
- Guides to free or low-cost outdoor activities like walking tours, biking routes, and parks.

Budget Tip:

- Check out BlogTO's **"Cheap Eats"** section for recommendations on budget-friendly restaurants and street food spots around Toronto.

Website: BlogTO

5. RedFlagDeals – Coupons and Local Discounts

RedFlagDeals is a Canadian website that focuses on finding and sharing deals, coupons, and promotions for everything from groceries to electronics. For budget travelers, it's a useful tool for finding discounts on dining, activities, and even transportation in Toronto.

What You Can Find:

- Coupons and discounts for local restaurants, cafes, and food delivery services.

- Deals on tickets to events, movie theaters, and attractions.
- Promotions for car rentals, hotels, and public transportation.

Budget Tip:

- Search for coupons or promotions for food delivery services like **UberEats** or **DoorDash**, which often offer discounts for first-time users or special deals on certain days of the week.

Website: RedFlagDeals

Saving Money on Groceries and Essentials in Toronto

1. Finding Affordable Grocery Stores

Toronto has many grocery store chains, but prices can vary depending on the location and the store. Here are some of the best options for budget travelers looking to save money on food.

No Frills

- **No Frills** is one of the most affordable grocery stores in Toronto, offering a wide range of products at lower prices than many other supermarkets. They focus on the essentials, and you'll find great deals on fresh produce, pantry staples, and frozen goods. If you're cooking your own meals, **No Frills** is a good place to stock up on affordable ingredients like pasta, rice, vegetables, and basic sauces.
- **What to buy:** Look for their **yellow price tags**, which indicate special discounts on items like fruits, vegetables, and dairy products.
- **Budget Tip:** They often have weekly specials, so it's worth checking their flyer (available online or in-store) before you go to take advantage of the best deals.
- **Location:** There are many locations across Toronto, including a central

one at **222 Lansdowne Ave, Toronto, ON M6K 3C6**.
- **How to get there:** Take the **504 King streetcar** or **47 Lansdowne bus** to **Lansdowne Ave**.

FreshCo

- Another budget-friendly option is **FreshCo**, a discount grocery store that offers low prices on fresh produce, meats, and dairy. It's similar to **No Frills**, but it's worth checking out both since their specials and sales can differ. **FreshCo** often has sales on bulk items and pantry staples, making it a good spot to grab food for several meals if you're staying for a longer period.
- **What to buy:** Fresh fruits and vegetables, canned goods, and bulk items like rice and beans.
- **Budget Tip:** Use FreshCo's price-match policy to get the best deal—if you find an item cheaper at a different grocery store, FreshCo will match the price.
- **Location:** One central location is **561 Sherbourne St, Toronto, ON M4X 1W6**.
- **How to get there:** Take the **Sherbourne subway station (Line 2)** and walk north to FreshCo.

Food Basics

Food Basics is a popular discount grocery chain with a good variety of fresh produce, meats, and dry goods at lower prices. It's known for offering great deals on bulk items and essentials like bread, milk, and cereal. The store's layout is simple, and while it may not have the gourmet selection of higher-end stores, it's perfect for travelers who are focused on keeping food costs down.

- **What to buy:** Bulk pantry items like pasta, grains, and canned goods.

Food Basics also has a great selection of discount bakery items and snacks.

- **Budget Tip:** Food Basics offers **bulk specials**—buying larger quantities of items like pasta, rice, and canned goods can save you a lot of money in the long run.
- **Location:** A central location is **830 Lansdowne Ave, Toronto, ON M6H 3Z3**.
- **How to get there:** Take the **Lansdowne subway station (Line 2)** and walk south to Food Basics.

2. Local Markets for Fresh and Affordable Produce

If you're looking for fresh produce at a great price, Toronto's local markets are the perfect place to shop. Many of these markets offer fresh fruits, vegetables, and even baked goods for less than you'd find at larger grocery chains.

Kensington Market

Kensington Market (Spadina Ave & Dundas St W) is one of the best spots in Toronto to find affordable produce and international ingredients. This vibrant neighborhood is filled with small grocery shops, fruit and vegetable stands, and specialty food stores. Prices are competitive, especially at the local vendors selling fresh fruits and vegetables.

- **What to buy:** Fresh fruits and vegetables, international spices, and pantry staples like rice and beans. Kensington Market also has specialty stores offering cheese, meats, and baked goods at reasonable prices.
- **Budget Tip:** The vendors at Kensington Market often reduce prices towards the end of the day, especially on weekends. Visit in the late afternoon for some of the best deals on fresh produce.
- **Location:** Spadina Ave & Dundas St W, Toronto
- **How to get there:** Take the **510 Spadina streetcar** to **Kensington Market**.

St. Lawrence Market

For fresh, high-quality produce and artisanal foods, head to **St. Lawrence Market** (93 Front St E). While the market has some higher-end offerings, there are also plenty of affordable vendors selling fresh fruits, vegetables, and baked goods. You can also find cheap eats like peameal bacon sandwiches and fresh bread, which are perfect if you're on the go.

- **What to buy:** Fresh fruits and vegetables, bread, and affordable snacks. If you're planning to cook, look for the butcher stalls where you can get good deals on fresh meats.
- **Budget Tip:** Visit early in the day for the best selection of fresh produce, or come later in the afternoon when vendors may offer discounts on items they want to sell before closing.
- **Location:** 93 Front St E, Toronto, ON M5E 1C3
- **How to get there:** Take the **King streetcar** to **Jarvis St**.

Chinatown Markets

Toronto's **Chinatown** (centered around Spadina Ave and Dundas St) is known for its budget-friendly grocery stores and street vendors. Here, you'll find fresh produce, Asian ingredients, and affordable meats and seafood. Chinatown is perfect for travelers looking to stock up on fresh ingredients without overspending.

- **What to buy:** Fresh vegetables, tofu, rice, and noodles. You can also find affordable cuts of meat and seafood at the local butcher shops.
- **Budget Tip:** Chinatown is one of the cheapest places in the city to buy fresh produce. If you're staying in Toronto for more than a few days, it's worth shopping here to keep your grocery costs down.
- **Location:** Spadina Ave & Dundas St W, Toronto
- **How to get there:** Take the **510 Spadina streetcar** to **Dundas St**.

3. Discount and Dollar Stores for Essentials

If you need to buy everyday essentials like toiletries, snacks, or cleaning supplies, Toronto has plenty of discount stores where you can find these items for less. Here are a few places to check out:

Dollarama

Dollarama is one of Canada's largest discount store chains, offering everything from snacks to cleaning supplies at very low prices. You'll find multiple locations across Toronto, and it's perfect for picking up small items like toothpaste, shampoo, or even non-perishable snacks like crackers and granola bars.

- **What to buy:** Toiletries, cleaning supplies, non-perishable snacks, and basic kitchenware (if you're staying in a place with a kitchenette).
- **Budget Tip:** Most items in Dollarama cost between **$1-4 CAD**, so it's one of the cheapest places to stock up on essentials.
- **Location:** One central location is **363 Yonge St, Toronto, ON M5B 1S1**.
- **How to get there:** Take the **Yonge-Dundas subway station (Line 1)** and walk to Yonge St.

Giant Tiger

Giant Tiger is a Canadian discount store that offers a wide variety of groceries, clothing, household goods, and basic essentials at very affordable prices. It's a great place to shop if you need groceries and a few other items, as they carry a bit of everything. You'll find everything from canned goods to personal care products at discounted prices.

- **What to buy:** Groceries like canned food, snacks, and frozen items, as well as essentials like laundry detergent and personal care products.
- **Budget Tip:** Giant Tiger often runs promotions on bulk items, so if you're staying in Toronto for a while, it's worth buying in larger quantities to save even more.

- **Location:** 404 Lansdowne Ave, Toronto, ON M6H 3Y1
- **How to get there:** Take the **Lansdowne subway station (Line 2)** and walk south to Giant Tiger.

4. Cooking on a Budget: Tips for Saving Even More

Cooking your own meals while traveling is one of the best ways to save money, especially if you're staying in accommodations with kitchen access. Here are some additional tips for keeping your food costs down while enjoying homemade meals:

Plan Your Meals Ahead:

- Before heading to the grocery store, plan out what you're going to cook for the week. Make a shopping list of ingredients you need and stick to it. This will help you avoid buying unnecessary items that can increase your food bill.

Cook in Bulk:

- If you're staying in Toronto for a few days, consider cooking larger portions of meals like pasta, stir-fries, or soups. You can store leftovers in the fridge and reheat them for the next day's lunch or dinner, which will save you both time and money.

Use Reusable Containers:

- If you're packing snacks or meals for day trips around the city, invest in reusable containers to store food. This will help you avoid buying takeout or overpriced snacks while you're out exploring.

Buy Store Brands:

- When shopping at discount grocery stores like **No Frills** or **Food Basics**, look for store-brand products. These are often just as good as name brands but at a lower price. Items like pasta, canned goods, and frozen vegetables are typically much cheaper if you buy the store-brand version.

5. **Essential Cooking Gear for Travelers**

If you're staying in an Airbnb or a hostel with kitchen access, you might not have all the cooking equipment you need. Here are some essentials that you can buy on a budget:

Basic Cookware and Utensils:

- Discount stores like **Dollarama** often sell basic kitchen items like pots, pans, spatulas, and cutting boards for **$1-4 CAD**. If you're staying for a while and cooking most of your meals, it's worth picking up a few items that you can leave behind when you leave the city.

Reusable Grocery Bags:

- Many grocery stores in Toronto charge **5 cents** per plastic bag, so bringing your own reusable bag can save you money. You can buy reusable bags at most grocery stores or discount stores like **Dollarama** for around **$1 CAD**.

6. **Final Budget Tips for Grocery Shopping in Toronto**

Compare Flyers:

- Most grocery stores in Toronto publish weekly flyers with deals and promotions. You can find these flyers online or in-store. Comparing flyers before you shop can help you find the best deals and save on essentials.

Buy in Season:

- Fruits and vegetables are cheaper when they're in season. Visit local markets like **Kensington Market** or **Chinatown** to buy fresh, seasonal produce at lower prices.

Avoid Convenience Stores:

- While convenience stores are handy, they usually charge more for basic items like snacks, drinks, and toiletries. Stick to grocery stores or discount stores like **Dollarama** and **Giant Tiger** to get better prices.

Essential Info

Emergency Contacts for Budget Travelers

1. Emergency Numbers in Toronto

For any emergencies while in Toronto, these are the most important numbers you'll need:

911 – Emergency Services (Police, Fire, Ambulance)

- In case of any emergency, dialing **911** will connect you to the police, fire department, or paramedics. This number is free to call from any phone, including payphones and cell phones, even if you don't have an active service plan.

Toronto Police Non-Emergency Number

For non-life-threatening situations or to report a crime after it has occurred, you can contact the **Toronto Police** non-emergency number at **416-808-2222**. This is useful if you need to report a stolen item, lost property, or suspicious activity that doesn't require immediate attention.

Toronto Fire Department Non-Emergency Number

If you need to contact the **Toronto Fire Department** for a non-emergency, such as a minor incident like a small fire or if you smell gas, you can call **416-338-9000**.

Toronto Public Health

If you need health-related information, such as advice on vaccinations, local outbreaks, or food safety, you can reach **Toronto Public Health** at **416-338-7600**. They provide useful information on public health matters and can guide you to local healthcare services.

2. Local Hospitals for Budget Travelers

If you encounter any health issues during your stay, Toronto has several hospitals and clinics that cater to travelers. Many hospitals offer emergency services and walk-in clinics for non-urgent medical needs.

Toronto General Hospital

- Located in the downtown core, **Toronto General Hospital** is one of the city's largest and most reputable medical centers. They have a 24/7 emergency department, and they offer world-class medical care for various issues.
- **Address:** 200 Elizabeth St, Toronto, ON M5G 2C4
- **Phone:** 416-340-3111
- **How to get there:** Take the **Line 1 subway** to **Queen's Park Station** and walk south.

St. Michael's Hospital

This is another central hospital that provides emergency medical services and general healthcare. It's located near downtown Toronto and is accessible by public transportation.

- **Address:** 30 Bond St, Toronto, ON M5B 1W8
- **Phone:** 416-360-4000
- **How to get there:** Take the **Line 1 subway** to **Queen Station** or the **King streetcar** to **Bond St**.

Mount Sinai Hospital

Mount Sinai is known for its excellent healthcare services, including emergency care. It's centrally located, making it convenient for travelers in the downtown area.

- **Address:** 600 University Ave, Toronto, ON M5G 1X5
- **Phone:** 416-596-4200
- **How to get there:** Take the **Line 1 subway** to **St. Patrick Station** and walk south.

Budget Tip:

For non-urgent care, consider visiting a **walk-in clinic** instead of an emergency room. Walk-in clinics are cheaper and quicker for minor health concerns like colds, minor injuries, or prescription refills. Some options include **Appletree Medical Group** (various locations, including **40 King St W**) and **Medcan Clinic** (150 York St, Toronto, ON M5H 3S5).

3. **Embassy Information for Travelers**

If you lose your passport, encounter legal issues, or need other consular assistance, it's important to know the location of your country's embassy or consulate in Toronto.

United States Consulate General

- **Address:** 360 University Ave, Toronto, ON M5G 1S4
- **Phone:** 416-595-1700
- **How to get there:** Take the **Line 1 subway** to **St. Patrick Station** and walk north.

British Consulate General

- **Address:** 777 Bay St, Suite 2800, Toronto, ON M5G 2G2
- **Phone:** 416-593-1290
- **How to get there:** Take the **Line 1 subway** to **College Station** and walk west.

Australian Consulate General

- **Address:** 175 Bloor St E, Suite 1901, Toronto, ON M4W 3R8
- **Phone:** 416-323-4280
- **How to get there:** Take the **Line 2 subway** to **Bloor-Yonge Station** and walk east.

Budget Tip:

- If you lose important documents like your passport, contact your embassy immediately. It's a good idea to keep digital copies of your passport and other travel documents in case they're lost or stolen.

4. Staying Informed in an Emergency

In case of an emergency or important updates (such as weather-related warnings), there are a few practical ways to stay informed as a traveler in Toronto.

Toronto Alert Ready System

Toronto uses the **Alert Ready System** to notify the public of emergencies. These alerts are sent to all smartphones, and they inform you of issues like severe weather, natural disasters, or public safety emergencies. Make sure your phone is turned on and has a local SIM card or roaming enabled so you can receive these alerts.

Local News Sources

Stay updated on local events and emergencies by following reliable local news outlets such as **CBC News Toronto** or **CP24**, which provide live updates on current events, including transportation delays or emergencies.

Toronto Police Twitter Account

The **Toronto Police Service Twitter** account (**@TorontoPolice**) provides real-time updates on road closures, police activity, and other emergencies. It's a helpful resource for knowing what's happening in the city.

5. Staying Safe in Toronto: Local Laws and Customs

Toronto is a welcoming and diverse city, but there are certain laws and customs you should be aware of to ensure you stay safe and avoid any misunderstandings or fines while traveling.

Local Laws for Budget Travelers
Alcohol Consumption

In Toronto, drinking alcohol in public spaces like parks, beaches, or streets is illegal unless you're in a designated area like a licensed patio or restaurant. Fines can range from **$100-500 CAD** for public drinking. Make sure to consume alcohol only in licensed establishments or private accommodations.

Budget Tip:

If you're staying at a hostel or Airbnb with kitchen access, buying alcohol from a **LCBO (Liquor Control Board of Ontario)** store and enjoying it at your accommodation is a more affordable option.

Public Transportation Rules

- Toronto's public transit system (TTC) has specific rules to ensure the safety and comfort of all riders. **Fare evasion** (riding without paying) is strictly enforced, and fines for not having a valid fare are **$235 CAD**. Make sure to always tap your **Presto card** or have a valid ticket before boarding the subway, bus, or streetcar.

Littering and Waste Disposal

- Littering in public spaces can lead to fines of up to **$500 CAD**. Toronto has strict waste disposal guidelines, and you'll find plenty of garbage bins and recycling stations throughout the city. Always dispose of your trash in designated areas.

Local Customs to Respect
Respect for Diversity

- Toronto is one of the most multicultural cities in the world, and it's important to respect the city's diversity. This includes being considerate of different cultures, religions, and languages. Treat people with kindness and avoid making assumptions based on their appearance or background.

Tipping Etiquette

- In Toronto, it's customary to tip servers in restaurants, bartenders, and taxi drivers. The standard tipping rate is **15-20%** of the total bill. If you're on a budget, it's helpful to factor this into your meal and transportation costs.

Crosswalk Laws

- Pedestrians in Toronto should be aware that it's illegal to jaywalk (cross the street outside of a designated crosswalk or intersection). Fines for jaywalking can range from **$35-50 CAD**. Always wait for the pedestrian light before crossing the street.

Cycling Laws

- Toronto is a bike-friendly city, but cyclists must follow certain rules. Helmets are mandatory for cyclists under **18**, and cyclists are required to follow the same traffic laws as cars. Always ride in designated bike lanes where available, and use hand signals when turning.

6. How to Stay Safe While Exploring the City

Toronto is a very safe city for travelers, but there are a few general safety tips to keep in mind, especially when traveling on a budget.

Stay in Well-Lit, Busy Areas

When walking around Toronto, especially at night, stick to well-lit and busy streets. Areas like **Queen Street West**, **Yonge Street**, and the **Distillery District** are safe to explore, even after dark. If you're unsure about a particular area, ask locals or check with your accommodation.

Avoid Scams and Tourist Traps

While Toronto is generally free of aggressive scams, it's still a good idea to stay alert. Be cautious of anyone approaching you asking for money or trying to sell you something on the street. If something seems too good to be true, it probably is. Stick to established stores and reputable vendors.

Budget Tip:

Toronto has plenty of safe and affordable areas to explore, like the **Toronto Islands**, **High Park**, and **St. Lawrence Market**. These places are not only budget-friendly but also attract a lot of locals and other travelers, making them safe and enjoyable spots to visit.

Emergency Assistance Apps

- Download helpful apps like **Google Maps** and **Citymapper** for navigating the city, and consider adding the **Red Cross First Aid** app for basic health and safety information. Having these tools can help you stay informed and safe as you explore Toronto.

Internet Access and Budget-Friendly SIM Cards

Staying connected is crucial when traveling, whether you need to navigate the city, contact friends or family, or access important travel details. Toronto offers plenty of free Wi-Fi options, and for longer stays or frequent data usage, getting an affordable SIM card is a smart way to stay online without racking up hefty roaming charges.

1. Free Wi-Fi in Toronto

Many public places and businesses in Toronto offer free Wi-Fi, making it easy for travelers to stay connected without purchasing a SIM card or data plan. Here are some of the best places to access free Wi-Fi throughout the city:

Toronto Public Libraries

All branches of the **Toronto Public Library** offer free Wi-Fi. With over 100 locations across the city, you're never far from a place where you can sit, relax, and connect to the internet for free. You don't need a library card to use the Wi-Fi, and libraries are great quiet spaces if you need to work, check emails, or just take a break.

- **Location:** One central location is **Toronto Reference Library**, 789 Yonge St, Toronto, ON M4W 2G8.
- **How to get there:** Take the **Line 1 subway** to **Bloor-Yonge Station**.

Cafés and Restaurants

Many cafés and fast-food restaurants in Toronto offer free Wi-Fi. Chains like **Starbucks**, **Tim Hortons**, and **McDonald's** provide free internet access for customers, and you'll find them in almost every neighborhood. Simply order a coffee or snack, and you can use their Wi-Fi for as long as you need.

- **Budget Tip:** Order something small, like a coffee or tea (typically **$2-3**

CAD), to make use of the free Wi-Fi without spending too much.

Public Parks and Squares

Certain public parks and squares in Toronto offer free Wi-Fi, particularly in popular areas. For example, **Nathan Phillips Square** (100 Queen St W, Toronto, ON M5H 2N2) and **Harbourfront Centre** (235 Queens Quay W, Toronto, ON M5J 2G8) provide free internet access. These outdoor spaces are ideal if you want to check directions, browse the web, or send messages while enjoying the city's atmosphere.

- **Location:** Nathan Phillips Square, 100 Queen St W
- **How to get there:** Take the **Line 1 subway** to **Queen Station**.

Shopping Malls

Large shopping malls like **Eaton Centre** (220 Yonge St, Toronto, ON M5B 2H1) offer free Wi-Fi throughout the complex. Whether you're shopping or just passing through, you can connect to the mall's internet and stay online while you browse stores or grab a quick meal.

- **Location:** 220 Yonge St, Toronto, ON M5B 2H1
- **How to get there:** Take the **Line 1 subway** to **Dundas Station**.

2. Budget-Friendly SIM Card Options

If you need constant internet access while traveling, purchasing a local SIM card is the best way to avoid expensive international roaming fees. Toronto has several options for affordable SIM cards that cater to budget-conscious travelers. Here's how you can get connected without breaking the bank:

Freedom Mobile

Freedom Mobile is one of the most affordable mobile providers in Toronto, offering budget-friendly prepaid plans. You can get a SIM card for around **$10 CAD**, and they have plans starting as low as **$25 CAD** per month. This includes unlimited local calls and texts and **1GB of data**, making it perfect for light usage. If you need more data, their **$35 CAD plan** gives you **6GB** of data.

- **Where to buy:** Freedom Mobile stores are located throughout Toronto, including a central location at **677 Yonge St, Toronto, ON M4Y 2B2**.
- **How to get there:** Take the **Line 1 subway** to **Wellesley Station**.

Chatr Mobile

Chatr is another budget-friendly option for prepaid SIM cards. They offer low-cost plans starting at **$25 CAD** per month, which includes unlimited local calling, texting, and **500MB of data**. You can add more data if needed, but for basic use like maps and messaging, this plan is great for budget travelers. SIM cards are also reasonably priced at **$10 CAD**.

- **Where to buy:** Chatr SIM cards are available at most convenience stores, mobile shops, and **Walmart** locations across Toronto. One central location is **Walmart at 900 Dufferin St, Toronto, ON M6H 4A9**.
- **How to get there:** Take the **Dufferin subway station (Line 2)** to **Dufferin Mall**.

Public Mobile

Public Mobile offers flexible prepaid plans that are ideal for travelers. Their basic plan starts at **$15 CAD** per month for **250MB of data**, unlimited texts, and 100 minutes of calling. You can buy their SIM cards online or at partner retailers like **The Mobile Shop** or **London Drugs**. Public Mobile's prices are among the most competitive in Canada, and their online platform allows you to manage your plan easily.

- **Where to buy:** You can purchase Public Mobile SIM cards at retailers like **The Mobile Shop** located inside **Loblaws** grocery stores. One central location is **60 Carlton St, Toronto, ON M5B 1J2**.
- **How to get there:** Take the **College subway station (Line 1)** and walk east.

Budget Tip: Buy a SIM card at the airport if you need immediate access to the internet upon arrival. Kiosks at **Toronto Pearson International Airport** offer prepaid SIM cards from various providers, though prices might be slightly higher than in the city.

3. Travel Insurance: Do You Need It for a Budget Trip?

Even though travel insurance might seem like an extra expense, it's an important consideration for budget travelers. While it's tempting to skip insurance to save money, unexpected situations—like medical emergencies, canceled flights, or lost luggage—can end up costing far more than the insurance itself. Here's why you should consider travel insurance and the types of coverage to look for.

Why Travel Insurance is Important

- Travel insurance provides protection against a wide range of potential issues that could arise during your trip. If you're traveling on a budget, the costs of unexpected events like hospital visits, lost baggage, or trip cancellations can quickly add up. With the right insurance, you can avoid these financial pitfalls and focus on enjoying your trip with peace of mind.
- For example, if you fall ill and need medical treatment while in Toronto, you could face steep medical bills if you don't have insurance. A simple visit to a hospital can cost hundreds of dollars, while more serious emergencies could cost thousands. Travel insurance will cover these costs, saving you from a financial burden.

Types of Travel Insurance to Consider

When choosing a travel insurance plan, consider the following coverage options, especially if you're a budget traveler:

- **Medical Coverage:** This is the most important type of coverage for any traveler. Medical insurance covers emergency medical expenses, such as doctor visits, hospital stays, and prescription medication. Look for a plan that offers at least **$100,000 CAD** in emergency medical coverage.
- **Trip Cancellation/Interruption:** If your trip is canceled or cut short due to unforeseen events (like illness, family emergencies, or weather), this coverage will reimburse you for any non-refundable travel expenses, such as flights and hotel bookings. It's especially useful if you've booked budget travel with strict no-refund policies.
- **Lost or Stolen Baggage:** Travel insurance can also cover the cost of replacing lost or stolen baggage. If you lose your luggage or it's delayed, your policy will reimburse you for essential items like clothing and toiletries.
- **Personal Liability:** Some travel insurance policies offer personal liability coverage, which protects you if you accidentally damage property or injure someone while traveling.
- **Budget Tip:** Shop around for travel insurance to find the best deal. Use comparison websites like **InsureMyTrip** or **World Nomads** to compare coverage and prices. Many insurance providers also offer short-term or single-trip plans, which can be more affordable than annual coverage.

Do You Need Travel Insurance for Canada?

- Canada has a public healthcare system, but it doesn't cover visitors or tourists. If you don't have travel insurance, you'll be responsible for paying out-of-pocket for any medical expenses. Therefore, it's highly recommended to have travel insurance with medical coverage, even for a short trip to Toronto.

ESSENTIAL INFO

Where to Buy Travel Insurance:

- You can buy travel insurance online through providers like **World Nomads, Allianz,** or **Manulife**. If you prefer to speak to someone directly, many travel agencies and insurance companies in Toronto can help you purchase coverage for your trip.
- **Cost:** The cost of travel insurance depends on the length of your trip, your age, and the level of coverage you choose. On average, budget travelers can expect to pay around **$50-100 CAD** for a short-term policy with comprehensive coverage.

4. Final Budget Tips for Staying Connected and Insured

- **Use Free Wi-Fi Strategically:** Plan your stops at places like libraries, cafes, and malls where you can use free Wi-Fi for essential tasks like navigating the city or contacting friends. This can help you save data on your SIM card for when you really need it.
- **Buy SIM Cards in the City:** While it's convenient to purchase SIM cards at the airport, prices are often higher. If you don't need immediate access to the internet, wait until you're in the city to buy a SIM card at a local mobile store or discount retailer.
- **Choose the Right Travel Insurance Plan:** Consider how long you'll be traveling and what kind of activities you'll be doing. If you're staying in Toronto for just a few days and don't plan on engaging in high-risk activities, you can opt for a basic plan with emergency medical and trip cancellation coverage. For longer trips, or if you're planning to visit multiple cities, a more comprehensive plan might be a better choice.

Conclusion

In wrapping up your journey through **Toronto On A Budget 2025**, you now have the tools and insights to explore one of Canada's most vibrant cities without stretching your budget. From free Wi-Fi hotspots to affordable SIM cards, budget-friendly attractions, and cost-saving tips for dining, transportation, and accommodation, Toronto offers a rich and rewarding experience for travelers who know where to look. By planning smartly, taking advantage of the city's many accessible resources, and keeping these practical tips in mind, you can fully immerse yourself in everything Toronto has to offer—without sacrificing comfort or enjoyment.

Whether you're exploring iconic landmarks, wandering through its diverse neighborhoods, or enjoying a meal at a local market, Toronto promises an unforgettable adventure that proves you don't need to spend a fortune to experience the best the city has to offer. Safe travels, and enjoy every budget-friendly moment in Toronto!

Printed in Great Britain
by Amazon